The Oldest Delegate

The Oldest Delegate

*Franklin in the
Constitutional Convention*

William G. Carr

DELAWARE

Newark: University of Delaware Press
London and Toronto: Associated University Presses

Associated University Presses
440 Forsgate Drive
Cranbury, NJ 08512

Associated University Presses
25 Sicilian Avenue
London WC1A 2QH, England

Associated University Presses
P.O. Box 488, Port Credit
Mississauga, Ontario
Canada   L5G 4M2

The paper used in this publication meets the requirements
of the American National Standard for Permanence of Paper
for Printed Library Materials Z39.48-1984.

Library of Congress Cataloging-in-Publication Data

Carr, William George, 1901–
    The Oldest delegate : Franklin in the Constitutional Convention /
William G. Carr.
      p.   cm.
    Includes bibliographical references.
    ISBN 0-87413-382-3 (alk. paper)
      1. Franklin, Benjamin, 1706–1790.   2. United States.
Constitutional Convention (1787)   3. United States—Constitutional
history.   4. United States—Politics and government—1783–1789.
I. Title.
E302.6.F8C34   1990
973.3'092—dc20   89-40211
                                                              CIP

PRINTED IN THE UNITED STATES OF AMERICA

So by living twelve years beyond David's period, I seem to have intruded myself into the company of posterity, when I ought to have been abed and asleep. Yet, had I gone at seventy, it would have cut off twelve of the most active years of my life, employed too in matters of greatest importance; and whether I have been doing good or mischief is for time to discover. I only know that I intended well and I hope all will end well.

—Franklin in 1788, age eighty-two

Contents

Preface

Events associated with the five-year Bicentennial of the United States Constitution (1987–92) provide an incentive to collate and evaluate information about the distinguished Americans who helped frame that historic document.

Biographers have offered a variety of opinions about the scope and importance of Benjamin Franklin's participation. He was, at eighty-one, by far the oldest delegate at the meeting of the federal convention in Philadelphia. Beyond that fact opinions differ and controversy continues.

Was his role that of a prolix patriarch, grudgingly endured because of his age and reputation, flattered regularly and followed rarely, occasionally amusing rather than consistently influential? Was he an impartial referee who everybody felt obliged to respect but not to heed as a serious collaborator? Was he a comic Methuselah in a sedan chair, feeble, garrulous, ineffective, and ignored? Was he capable of identifying and suggesting solutions to contentious issues? Or was his influence due mostly to his presence and fame? Did his age and frailty impair his ability to function as a deputy for Pennsylvania?

With few exceptions, the convention delegates were men of high competence and devotion. Some of them have been exalted by historians as indispensable men, absolutely necessary to success. For instance, James Madison earned the title "Father of the Constitution" through his brilliant mind, unflagging zeal, and copious notes. George Washington, too, though his formal participation was limited to presiding over some of the meetings, lent dignity to the convention and credibility to its proposals.

However, Benjamin Franklin, although acknowledged for his immense public services during the Revolutionary War, has usually been relegated to a minor role in 1787. The facile explanation for this conclusion is Franklin's age and frailty. Yet, in light of the record gathered in this book, the denigration of Franklin's role is difficult to justify or to accept.

Having earned my bread and butter mainly by attending na-

9

tional and international conferences, and being, of late, often the senior participant at such gatherings, I hope in the following pages to offer a reasonably complete description of Franklin's part in the Constitutional Convention.

Acknowledgments

First among those I wish to thank are my colleagues on the Board of Governors of the Benjamin Franklin Guild who encouraged me to assail the subject of this book.

Members of the board who have given the most explicit help include Frank B. Jones, president of the Guild; Robert Haynes, Western Kentucky University; Leo Lemay, University of Delaware; and Fred Schwengel, U.S. Capitol Historical Society.

To President Jones I am especially grateful. He patiently and critically reviewed each successive draft in manuscript, suggested points of revision, shepherded me cheerfully through the Franklin memorabilia in Philadelphia, included me in two helpful conferences at Indiana University, lent me hard-to-get reference books, suggested and supplied much useful reading material, and assisted in locating a publisher.

With grace and good nature, Mrs. Katherine B. Watson has met every request in typing the numerous textual revisions—a process greatly facilitated by her skill in handling a word processor. She has, in addition, helped far beyond the usual expectations by her practical suggestions regarding the clarity and accuracy of the text.

My thanks are also extended to Hobart Cawood, director, and David Dutcher and David Kimball, historians, at Independence National Historical Park. Mr. Kimball in particular provided in 1987 a review of one of the earlier drafts. Jeanne Roberts, Historical Society of Pennsylvania, and Martin Levitt, American Philosophical Society, have also contributed information.

Of all the people who have helped, none bears any responsibility for such errors of fact and opinion as my incorrigibility has allowed to persist in these pages.

The Oldest Delegate

1
Evaluations

In February 1787 the Continental Congress summoned a meeting of delegates from the thirteen states to a convention. Their assignment: to render the Articles of Confederation "adequate to the exigencies of Government and the preservation of the union." Rhode Island officially ignored the summons but the other twelve states responded—some were slow, others prompt; some deeply concerned, others perfunctory.

Most people readily agreed that the existing government was ineffective, but the remedial measures required produced sharp and wide-ranging disputes.

The convention was called to meet in Philadelphia on 14 May. However, response was so lethargic and travel so difficult that no quorum was present until 28 May. Thereafter deliberations continued—as a rule, five hours a day, six days a week—until 17 September. On that day a draft constitution was sent to Congress to be ratified by conventions in each state.

The resulting document has defined how the United States and its people have been governed for the past two centuries. During that long period, the Constitution has been constantly examined by the people, often interpreted by the federal courts, and occasionally amended by a proccess that the Constitution itself describes. It has remained "the Supreme Law of the Land."

By its own rules, the convention debates were kept secret. Fortunately the extensive daily notes by James Madison, together with shorter records written by others, provide a good summary of the course of debates and the remarks by individual delegates.

Since the day the Constitutional Convention adjourned, the significance of its work and the value of the contributions by the active delegates such as Benjamin Franklin have remained of lively interest to public leaders and professional historians.

The eighty-one-year-old Benjamin Franklin was one of the most eminent convention delegates. This opening chapter traces

some of the evaluations of his role as recorded during the inter-
vening years.

JOHN ADAMS

John Adams grudgingly admired Franklin's ability and jealously
detested his conduct. On 4 April 1790, the newly elected (and
first) vice president of the United States bitterly derided Franklin's
role in the revolution and in the government generally. While,
unknown to him, Franklin lay dying in Philadelphia, Adams expressed his feelings of persecution and suspicion in a letter to the
patriot and social reformer, Dr. Benjamin Rush, in the same city:
"The history of our Revolution will be one continuous Lye from
one end to the other. The essence of the whole will be that Dr.
Franklin's Rod smote the earth and out sprung General Washington. That Franklin electrified him with his rod—and thence-
forth these two conducted all the Policy, Negotiations, Legislatures
and War" (quoted in Stourzh 1969, 262).

During the two centuries since Adams's strictures, the attitude
among historians toward Franklin's role in the convention has
improved—but not much. The kindest thing that most of them
can say about his influence is that the views of the convention's
oldest and most prestigious delegate were generally ignored.

LATER COMMENTS

For instance, David Schoenbrun disposes briskly of Franklin's
role in the Convention: "The Constitution was drafted with only
minor contributions by . . . the sick old man" (1976, 394).
Seymour Block (1975, 355) adds that, although the old man received personal respect, "the Convention belonged to the younger
men who paid little attention to most of his proposals." A more
explicit statement of the same conclusion is provided by Lyon
(1936, 73): "The young men who made a huge majority of the
Convention regarded the aged savant and statesman [Franklin] as
somewhat of a bother. . . ."

A 1986 book on the Constitutional Convention gives considerable attention to the personalities and characteristics of four of the
"most remarkable" delegates. Madison is described as "one of
America's keenest political thinkers." Washington "defeated the
world's mightiest fighting force . . . and would go on to run a

model presidency." Hamilton is remarkable because he "would in large measure design the American economic system." Franklin concludes the list; he is described as "old and infirm, but nonetheless considered by all one of the great men of his time." (Collier and Collier 1986, 170–71).

It is true, as Thomas Fleming writes, that on such radical proposals as a single-house legislature, Franklin's opinions were "largely ignored" (1972, 484). However, a major convention issue—perhaps indeed the major obstacle to agreement—was the basis for the representation of the states in Congress. This issue very nearly caused the convention to fail. Yet the solution was successfully supported and advocated by Franklin, who realized it could be applied *only* in a bicameral legislature.[1]

The most severe disparagement of Franklin's role in the Convention occurs in the biography by the French historian, Bernard Fay. He concludes that throughout the sessions of the convention, Franklin advocated "lost causes" and "praised the French liberalism in which no one was interested" (1929, 504). On point after point, says Fay, Franklin's suggestions were rebuffed or ignored; the convention and Franklin "did not talk the same language." Indeed, Fay asserts flatly that during the last half of the convention Franklin "no longer participated in the session except to propose or support compromises." Fay calls Franklin's role in the Constitutional Convention "political suicide; he had helped to organize a regime which was different from what he . . . had been recommending for thirty years, and he had put a group of men in power who had no confidence in him. He knew it and they made him feel it" (1929, 505).

In 1913, as the culmination of extended research, the American historian Max Farrand published his account of the framing of the Constitution. In one section he names the delegates who in his opinion contributed most to the work. He assigns first place to Madison, "unquestionably the leading spirit," "the master-builder of the Constitution," and "pre-eminent." Farrand's opinion on Madison's role has been influential. Indeed, one subsequent writer on the subject (Frank Donovan) entitled his book *Mr. Madison's Constitution*, thus awarding Madison a sole proprietorship, which the shy, soft-spoken, industrious little man, when living, had denied promptly and vigorously.

A close second to Madison, according to Farrand, was James Wilson of Pennsylvania. Third in his list is Washington. After naming eight other influential delegates, Farrand adds (1913, 199): "It may seem surprising that no particular mention is made of Benjamin Franklin. It must be remembered that Franklin was at the time a very old man, so feeble that Wilson read all of his speeches for him and while he was highly respected his opinions do not seem to have carried much weight."

In a later work Farrand explained that Franklin did not take an important part in the convention and that "his powers were failing" (1921, 113).

Farrand's generalization that Franklin addressed the Convention only by speeches written in advance and read by James Wilson seems to be based on an impression recalled, nearly a half century later, by James Madison. Retired to private life after eight years as secretary of state and two full terms as president, Madison by that time was himself over eighty. Madison's memory after nearly fifty years should be contrasted with his own *Notes* written daily in the course of the convention.

These *Notes* contain several important statements by Franklin that were not read for him by Wilson or by anyone else, remarks that seem to have been extemporaneous and, in some cases, must have been so under the circumstances described. In 1829 Madison himself, in an interview with historian Jared Sparks, said that although Franklin's speeches were "generally written," Franklin would occasionally "make short extemporaneous speeches with great pertinency and effect" (Farrand 1966, 3:481).

Ranking delegates for their value to the Constitution depends in part on what one regards as most important about that document. Irving Brant (1950, 159), for instance, estimates that "Madison and Franklin contributed more than any others to the trend of the Convention toward popular self-government."

The Mitchells (1964, 47), after a review of all delegates, mention eight as "of the first order of ability": Hamilton, Franklin, Madison, Mason, the two Morrises, Washington, and Wilson.

However, unlike some other students of the convention, who seem content to record only that feeble Franklin was by far the oldest delegate, the Mitchells call him "the Nestor of the meeting" (1964, 64)—an appellation that implies not only that he was old and experienced but also that he was wise.

COMPREHENSIVE ESTIMATES

Clinton Rossiter—writing on the role of Alexander Hamilton in the drafting, ratification, and application of the Constitution—omits Hamilton (with obvious regret) from his list of "the truly useful men" at Philadelphia. Rossiter's list includes James Madison, James Wilson, Gouverneur Morris, Roger Sherman, John Rutledge, Oliver Ellsworth, Rufus King, Franklin, and Washington. Rossiter, who wryly describes Franklin as "the patron saint of science, savings banks, volunteer fire companies, and a free press" (1964, 4), also notes that Franklin's endorsement was among the key factors that led to success in Hamilton's campaign to secure New York's almost essential unconditional ratification in July 1788 (1964, 69).

Merrill Jensen has conducted extensive research on colonial and early American history and has described brilliantly the emergence of various ideas during the constitutional debates. In addition Jensen traced (1964, 38) the contributions of twelve men identified as "key figures in the Convention." This group includes three strongly "nationalist" delegates (Madison, Wilson, Gouverneur Morris); four who in general wished merely to modify in varying degrees the provisions of the Articles of Confederation (Sherman, Paterson, Gerry, and Luther Martin), and four "middle" men (Mason, Dickinson, Ellsworth, Rutledge). The twelfth man in Jensen's list is George Washington, who presided in silent dignity over the formalities of the convention and offered for the record no significant opinions. Franklin is scarcely mentioned in the work and is not included among Jensen's "key figures." He becomes the convention's eminent, genial, and invisible man.

A few more recent articles assess Franklin's role more completely and favorably. Thus, Commager's 1987 essay on "The Achievement of the Framers" explains that the eighteenth century philosophical trend known as the Enlightenment manifested itself in different forms in the New World and in Europe. The changing tide of thought questioned tradition, celebrated reason, proclaimed the possibility of universal progress, respected the individual, and applied empirical methods. In the Old World its proudest triumphs were such scientific and artistic monuments as Newton's *Principia,* the architecture of Versailles, and the music of "Don Giovanni." In America, by contrast, the energy of the Enlightenment was applied to social welfare, law, economics, and government. "Franklin was its symbol," concludes Commager, and the Constitution and the Bill of Rights its greatest glory.

Federalism, Commager declares, may be considered as "the most successful and enduring contribution of the Convention." And if Madison is considered "the father of the Constitution," Franklin is "the father of Federalism." The title is justified by Franklin's 1754 draft of the "Albany Plan of Union" and his 1775 draft of "The Articles of Confederation and Perpetual Union," documents that anticipated the federal republic of 1787 by thirty-three and twelve years, respectively.

REFERENCE WORKS

Commonly-used reference books may provide a useful summary of the current views of historians on Franklin.

The *Concise Dictionary of American Biography* (312) tells us that "none of his [Franklin's] cardinal ideas was accepted, but his personality and genial humor proved invaluable in soothing tempers and in suggesting compromises."

The article on "Constitution" in the *Dictionary of American History* (Scribner's, vol. 2) speaks of "the aged, garrulous, but vastly prestigious Benjamin Franklin." (Aged he was and prestigious, but *garrulous?*)

Finally the new *Encyclopedia of the American Constitution* (Levy, ed.) presents a more detailed but essentially similar summary:

> At the Constitutional Convention Franklin was a conciliator and mediator. Although at 81 he was in failing health and had to have his speeches read . . . Franklin attended almost all sessions. Such proposals as he put forth (e.g. unicameral legislation, plural executive, elected judges, unpaid officials) were too radical to attract much support, but Franklin, with his humorous anecdotes and his commitment to the Union, served the Convention well by cooling tempers and encouraging compromises.

SUMMARY

To such generalizations, a double response is necessary. First, productive agreement following prudent compromise *was* one of Franklin's "cardinal ideas." Second, this idea and many others proposed or supported by Franklin *were* accepted at Philadelphia and, as we shall see, are now embodied in the Constitution.

Franklin, from the very outset of the convention, personified the spirit of goodwill that was essential to avoid the collapse of the entire effort. His fellow delegates *elected* him to the crucial Committee on Compromise. In doing so they must have thought either that compromise was impossible and membership on the committee was not important, *or* that Franklin had unusual objectivity, commitment, and persuasiveness. And if the first explanation is at variance with the record, the triumphant solution confirms the second explanation.

The esteem that other delegates felt for Franklin is shown by the convention records right up to the final session. When the last vote was to be taken, the form of the motion was carefully designed to reduce to a minimum the number of dissenting votes. This near unanimity would, it was hoped, help to bring about ratification of the Constitution in the several states. Hence, a form of words was designed by Gouverneur Morris with this aim in view. Why did not Morris himself offer the motion he had drafted? Because it was agreed to ask Franklin to introduce Morris' motion, "that it might have the better chance of success" (Madison 1966, 654).

Although he failed to secure majority approval of some of his specific proposals, Franklin was often on the winning side. He helped to avert provisions for an *absolute* presidential veto. He played for time on the proposal to establish a federal judiciary and ultimately a clause on federal courts was included in the Constitution. He argued effectively for a relatively short naturalization process for immigrants. He was outspoken in urging that the Constitution provide a process for the impeachment and removal from office of federal officials, up to and including the president. He repeatedly, and in the end successfully, opposed several efforts to limit the national suffrage and access to public office. He helped make conviction of treason more difficult and the right of dissent more secure.

Above all, when he was not fitting keys to deadlocks, he was concentrating on the main issue—the urgent need for a strong, efficient, central government; a government in which the people could participate; one with built-in deterrents to tyranny and corruption. This oldest statesman of the youngest republic symbolized the continuity of the revolutionary principles and democratic aspirations of the Declaration of Independence.

Franklin in 1787 was indeed old and occasionally in pain, but he was not yet dead. His mind was clear, his experience richly varied, his thoughts rational, and his ablities to express those opinions superb. Ignored on some issues, out-voted on others, successful on still others, Franklin served ably on the convention's most important committee, the last-chance committee on Compromise, to offer and defend an acceptable solution when hope for any agreement at all was only a guttering candle.

This conciliatory function, exercised in a cockpit of controversy, has been noticed by nearly all historians of the Constitutional

Convention, even by those who are chiefly absorbed in their concern about Franklin's frailty and advanced age.

Some of these writers also take note of a second function—Franklin's symbolic role as the nation's best-known citizen, second only to George Washington in public esteem. He assisted the convention just by being there, lending his optimism and courage to all of his younger colleagues.

As the present examination of Franklin's role continues, it will include a third, and hitherto largely neglected, contribution—Franklin's successful defense of the right and duty of people to participate in an efficient form of popular government.

2
Places and People

PHILADELPHIA

"Dear Philadelphia," as Franklin sometimes called it when he had been away a long time, was the new nation's largest city, its cultural center and chief seaport.

The convention met from 25 May to 17 September in the Pennsylvania State House, a public building now called Independence Hall. By today's standards for conference procedures, the schedule of meetings would surely be called grueling. There is not a single recorded lunch break or even a ten-minute coffee break.

A delegate from Connecticut, William Samuel Johnson, kept unusually detailed expense accounts and a daily weather log. The latter described thirty-seven days in July and August, as "warm," "hot," and "very hot." It was, in brief, a typical Philadelphia summer. Considering the absence of mechanical cooling and the prevailing fashions in men's attire, the delegates may be said to have "sweated out" the Constitution.

One wonders how the young delegates to their young country's most important political assembly occupied their time when the convention was not in session. What could claim their attention during the intervals between daily sessions and on days when only small committees met? They could talk together about the issues arising during the sessions, but they could not, under their rules, discuss the substance of their meetings with any except other delegates. They could shop (while their money held out) in Philadelphia's varied well-stocked shops, visit Charles Willson Peale's Museum and Art Gallery, inspect his portraits of notables and his wife's growing collection of fossils, visit Dr. Chavett's wax museum, leaf through any of the town's dozen or so thin newspapers, write their letters, compile their expense accounts, call on friends (if they had any in the area), visit the public gardens or historic colonial sites, go to church, attend the limited schedule of cultural events, read books from the Library Company in Carpenter's

Hall, hunt and fish, eat and drink, play billiards, chess, or cards, attend horse races or cockfights.

During the recently concluded war, partly as an economy measure and partly as a Presbyterian gesture, the municipal government banned theatrical productions. The rule was in effect until 1789. Plays could be presented outside the city or they could be disguised as "moral lectures" or "spectacles." *Hamlet* could appear as a lecture on "filial piety" or *Richard III* as a dissertation "on the fate of tyrants" (Peters 1987, 46). In 1784 a troupe of professional actors from London had arrived in Philadelphia but it soon moved to the brighter prospects of New York City.

Franklin regarded his Philadelphia social scene with satisfaction. To Polly Hewson[1] in 1786, hoping she would emigrate to America, he wrote:

> Cards we sometimes play here, not for money but for honour or the pleasure of defeating one another. . . . We have neither plays nor operas but we had yesterday a kind of oratorio . . . and we have assemblies, balls, and concerts besides little parties at one another's houses in which there is sometimes dancing. . . . In London you have plays performed by good actors. That, however, is the only advantage." (Van Doren 1938, 737).

Safety at night was increased by such unusual comforts as paved and lighted streets, an alert volunteer fire brigade, and a regular watch to patrol the neighborhood. The younger delegates might be pleased and perhaps astonished to find such comforts in the convention city. It is very doubtful, however, that any of them would know, or care, that these and other urbanities had been developed mainly by the enterprise of their distinguished host and colleague, Doctor Benjamin Franklin.

Some people, nevertheless, feared for other reasons to reside in Philadelphia. It certainly was not a health resort. Erastus Wolcott of Connecticut declined the honor of serving as a delegate because he would not "hazard his life" in a Philadelphia summer. Daniel Carroll of Maryland bravely attended the sessions in the city but lived in Germantown because it was "healthy, and a suitable distance" (about five miles) from city hazards. Elbridge Gerry of Massachusetts moved his young wife and infant daughter out of their rented Philadelphia house on Spruce Street and packed them off to live with relatives in a safer New York City. That summer, indeed, a mysterious epidemic swiftly took the lives of many Philadelphia children (Hutson 1987).

THE INDIAN QUEEN

One of the best taverns in North America was the Indian Queen, a well-known establishment where many of the delegates had stayed on previous visits. Jefferson, it is believed, stayed there in 1776 although he moved elsewhere to draft the Declaration of Independence. The Indian Queen was, presumably, named to honor Pocahontas, whose encounter with Captain John Smith was a popular episode in colonial history. There were Indian Queen taverns in at least six other states.

Guests at the *Indian Queen* included several Virginia delegates who were rewarded for arriving on time by first choice of quarters. "We are very well accommodated," George Mason wrote with evident satisfaction, "have a good room to ourselves, and are charged only 25 Pennsylvania currency per day, including our servants and horses, exclusive of club or liquors."

Satisfied as he was with his lodgings, the master of Gunston Hall took a strong dislike to other aspects of Philadelphia's urban and urbane social customs. Within his first week of residence, Mason was already vexed by the wining and dining formalities of fashionable society. "It is impossible to judge how long we shall be detained here," he complained. "I begin to grow heartily tired of the etiquette and nonsense. . . . It would take me some months to make myself master of them, and that it should require months to learn what is not worth remembering as many minutes . . . determines me to give no manner of trouble about them" (quoted from Mason's *Collected Papers* in Miller, 1975, 235). This, it should be noted, was Mason's first and last trip away from Virginia; other delegates with more experience of travel may not have felt a similar aggravation.

Later arrivals at the *Indian Queen* included John Rutledge and Charles Pinckney of South Carolina; Caleb Strong and Nathaniel Gorham of Massachusetts; William Pierce of Georgia; Alexander Hamilton of New York; Alexander Martin and Hugh Williamson of North Carolina.

When Manasseh Cutler as a concerned observer visited the city during the 1787 Convention, he described the *Indian Queen* as "a large pile of buildings with many spacious halls, and numerous small apartments." Its location between Market and Chestnut was near the center of the city; in fact, the inn's stable yard adjoined Franklin's Philadelphia property. Cutler found the establishment "kept in an elegant style" (Farrand 1966, 3:58). The servants were liveried (Collier and Collier 1986, 45).

The Pennsylvania delegates, including Franklin, remained at their respective homes in town. Washington was the welcomed guest in the comfortable home of Robert and Mary Morris. Johnson and others stayed at the City Tavern.

A group of the delegates could nearly always be readily assembled at the *Indian Queen*. The tavern became a center for social gatherings. These included an 11 June organized reception for delegates, and a 2 July dinner in honor of Thomas McKean, chief justice of Pennsylvania. Franklin and Washington were especially and formally invited to such events.

THE DELEGATES

To serve as a delegate to the "Federal Convention" was in many cases regarded as an onerous duty rather than an opportunity to achieve distinction or to render a public service. The twelve participating republics named a total of seventy-four representatives for the meeting. More than one-fourth of them never appeared in Phildelphia. Of the fifty-five men who did deposit their credentials and attend some of the sessions, only forty-two stayed to the end. Thirty-nine of these signed the Constitution, and three refused to do so.

Franklin, unlike the many delegates who did not appear or who attended only briefly, readily accepted public responsibility. His self-proclaimed rule for such appointments was "never ask, never refuse, never resign." He varied from this rule very few times in his long life. Nothing in the record suggests that he felt burdened or distressed by the added duties of the convention or that he would have escaped them if he could.

To picture Franklin in action as a convention delegate, one must consider that he was also in other respects a very busy man.

As president of the Pennsylvania Supreme Executive Council, he took part in many of the council's frequent meetings, administrative, deliberative and ceremonial, including its relations to the Pennsylvania State Assembly. He was an active president of the American Philosophical Society, the Society for Political Enquiries, and the Society for the Abolition of Slavery. He was a member of the City Council and a trustee of the University of Pennsylvania. He had to meet important visitors to the city, and often entertained them, with some of the delegates, at dinner or tea in his home. He conducted an extensive correspondence with scientists, writers, and politicians in America, England, and France.

On the personal side, he had just completed supervising some construction and fireproofing at his home; in fact, during the convention, he paid the final landscaping bill. And he was at the same time overseeing the remodeling of other residential properties he owned in his neighborhood.

Like many other old men at meetings, Franklin missed the comrades of earlier years who were now indifferent, incapacitated, retired, or dead. Many aspects of the convention intensified his loss of the old familiar faces. The most obvious one was his advanced age, but almost equally important in the Philadelphia of 1787 were his extended absence from the country, his lack of military service in the revolution, and his very limited formal schooling.

MILITARY EXPERIENCE

Of the other delegates, nearly two-thirds shared the cohesive experience of service in the Continental Army or state militias (U.S. Army 1986). Their ranks ranged from commander-in-chief (Washington) and brigadier-general (Dickinson, Mifflin, and Charles Cotesworth Pinckney) to Lieutenant (Charles Pinckney). One of them (Williamson) had been a surgeon, and one (Baldwin) a chaplain in the Continental Army.

Franklin had often served his country in hardship posts as a civilian, but his military experience was brief, remote in time, and narrow in scope. Back in 1747 during King George's War against France and Spain, Franklin assisted in organizing the defense of Pennsylvania.

Again in 1755, during the Indian Wars, Franklin wrote the legislation that created and funded the Pennsylvania militia. He commanded a militia campaign in Northampton County, and was elected colonel of his Philadelphia unit. The military exercises associated with this distinction had been at times burdensome to Franklin's essentially civilian nature. When the regiment exuberantly fired a ceremonial salvo before its colonel's front door, he complained that the concussion "shook down and broke several glasses of my electrical apparatus." He claimed with apparent pride to be "totally ignorant of military ceremonies." He ordered his mounted military escorts to keep their swords sheathed "without hurting or even terrifying man, woman, or child." He was averse "to making show or parade or doing any useless thing that can serve only to excite envy" (Van Doren 1938, 254).

Franklin was, it seems, during his brief colonial military career, an efficient and considerate administrative officer, but he was never at home in a military environment. And, although he approved of its support for strong national unity, he actively disliked some of the original ideas of the Society of the Cincinnati, an officers' veteran organization. Although he did not share their sectarian doctrines, Franklin outspokenly admired the Pennsylvania Quakers and often supported the Quaker Party. Franklin was thus separated, by both inexperience and sentiment, from the high spirits of men attending an old soldiers' reunion.

OCCUPATION AND SCHOOLING

Many delegatees followed more than one occupation; their chief primary vocations included thirty-four lawyers and ten planters. "B. Franklin, Printer," however, was neither lawyer nor planter. He, almost alone, represented the skilled trades.

Because of his many writings and his extensive activities as publicist and publisher, Franklin may also be regarded as the convention's only representative of the Fourth Estate. He issued the first public announcement of the general nature of the government recommended by the convention.

Few of the delegates could be considered, as the phrase went, "of humble origin." By modern standards for making such judgments, the delegates cannot be described as a cross section of the American people. Franklin, no less than the others, would probably have felt somewhat puzzled, perhaps affronted, if he had heard himself thus described. He would certainly have been astounded to learn that anyone would regard such a cross section desirable or necessary in the selection of delegates to draft a constitution.

In an era when few people acquired more than primary schooling, over half of the delegates had attended college. Furthermore, higher education in those days was a severely selective privilege. Just to *enter* King's College (now Columbia University), for example, required that a young man in his middle teens not only possess a "blameless moral character," but also be able to translate the *Aeneid* from Latin into English and the *Gospel of Saint John* from Greek into Latin (MacDonald, 1985, chapter 1).

Although records are incomplete regarding the youth and education of some of the delegates, the following partial summary shows the extent of their education in American colleges. Four (Baldwin, Ingersoll, Johnson, and Livingston) graduated from Yale; three (King, Gerry, and Strong) from Harvard; two (Blair and Randolph) from William and Mary; two (Hamilton and Gouverneur Morris) attended King's College; two (Mifflin and Williamson) were alumni of the University of Pennsylvania; and at least eight (Bedford, Brearly, Dayton, Ellsworth, Houstoun, Luther Martin, Madison, Paterson) attended the College of New Jersey, (Princeton). In addition C. C. Pinckney graduated from Christ Church College, Oxford; Spaight and Wilson attended Glasgow University; Williamson enrolled in the Medical School in Utrecht; and Carroll in the Jesuit College of St. Omers in Flanders.

Modern academic accounting systems would calculate an immense gap between the mere two years of Franklin's formal primary schooling and the tutors, academies, and universities of most other delegates. The oldest delegate was in fact the least-schooled, and the most broadly educated, member of the Convention. Franklin's array of English, Scottish, and American honorary degrees, combined with his lifetime of publications, scientific achievements, technical inventions, and political insight, restored the balance. The oldest delegate could take whatever satisfaction he wished by noticing (and it is warrantable he *did* notice!) that he was usually addressed as "Doctor Franklin."

The delegates who had the advantages of a rigorous classical higher education were, nevertheless and in general, the elite of the American population, "well-bred, well-fed, well-read, and (most of them) well-wed" (Burns 1982, 40).

BIRTHPLACE AND TRAVELS

Delegates who were born abroad included James McHenry, Thomas Fitzsimmons, William Paterson, and Pierce Butler in Ireland; Robert Morris and William Davie in England; James Wilson in Scotland; Alexander Hamilton in Nevis, West Indies. The remaining delegates were, like Franklin, native-born. Some delegates, again like Franklin, had been born into the first generation of immigrants. Many others (Bedford, Blount, Brearly, Carroll, Gilman, Gorham, Langdon, Mifflin) were scions of distinguished families, long-established in America.

The places of birth and residence became important to many young delegates when, during the convention, the constitutional provisions for eligibility to federal offices were considered. To Franklin, however, these personal considerations were irrelevant.

More important than birthplace was the value of extended travel experience. In this, Franklin was in a class by himself. His years of residence and public service in London and Paris, his visits to England, Scotland, Ireland, Holland, Madeira, Belgium, and Germany, his diplomatic journeys to Canada, and his official travels as postmaster throughout the entire country made Franklin by far the most traveled delegate at the convention and probably the most extensively traveled American of his time.

The advantages of observant travel, however extensive, were not automatically valuable in the Constitutional Convention. Of the previous thirty years, Franklin could count sixteen years in England, nine years in Paris, and only five years in Philadelphia. Although on missions abroad he had met, made, and kept a host of new friends in the Old World, few American friends visited London or Paris, and such visits were usually brief.

Thus, if he glanced at the growing list of convention delegates due to arrive in Philadelphia, Franklin saw the names of a few old friends, a few old opponents (mostly still old friends, nevertheless, or Friends) and many names quite unknown or known only by reputation or rumor. As he himself ruefully observed, he had been so long abroad as to be "almost a stranger in my own country" (Van Doren 1938, 718). It was an obstacle, quite apart from his age, which he had to and would overcome.

COLLEAGUES OF '76

Only seven delegates to the Constitutional Convention were known to Franklin as cosigners of the Declaration of Independence. For these eight men the convention might be regarded as a kind of reunion, meeting daily in the very room where they had mutually pledged their lives and fortunes only eleven eventful years earlier.

A meeting like the federal convention would partially satisfy the natural longing of most old people to encounter old friends (or even old foes?) and, with memory's aid, relive the good old days and deplore the modern lapses.

Two of the most distinguished among the Declaration signers were now in key diplomatic posts in Europe. Thomas Jefferson was in Paris as a successor (he insisted that no one call him a "replacement") of Benjamin Franklin. In London, John Adams was Minister at the Court of Saint James.

FRANKLIN'S FRIENDS

Before the convention met, Franklin was acquainted with about eighteen delegates. Seven Pennsylvanians led this list, followed by two delegates each from Connecticut, Virginia, and neighboring Delaware, and one each from Massachusetts, New Hampshire, New Jersey, North Carolina, and South Carolina.

George Clymer, Pennsylvania, an unassuming but highly esteemed Philadelphia merchant, had been an early and reliable champion of separation from Britain. He joined Franklin and Wilson in signing the Declaration of Independence.

John Dickinson, Delaware, had a long and varied association with Franklin. Born in Maryland, growing up in Pennsylvania and Delaware, Dickinson studied law in Philadelphia and at the Middle Temple in London. In 1764 at the Pennsylvania Assembly, he unsuccessfully opposed Franklin on the issue of changing the Penn family proprietorship into a royal province (Morse, 1899, 96–97). In 1767 Dickinson opposed British tax policy in his *Letters from a Pennsylvania Farmer,* Franklin contributing a preface for the English edition.

In 1775 the two served on the Pennsylvania Committee of Safety and the Committee on Secret Correspondence to consult with potential allies abroad. This initiative led to the assignment of Franklin as a representative to France. Nevertheless, the two differed over the issue of independence. Dickinson, driven perhaps by family pressures, drafted the "Olive Branch" petition to the king, pleading for better treatment. The olive branch thus extended, although formally endorsed by the Continental Congress, was disapproved by delegates Adams, Jefferson, and Franklin. It was ignored by that British government to which it was so humbly addressed.

Even in 1776, Dickinson did not sign the Declaration, being cautiously uncertain that the break with Britain was irreparable.

In 1785, following Franklin's return from Paris, and his election as President of the Pennsylvania Supreme Executive Council (succeeding Dickinson), the two found an occasion for cooperation. They made a joint, and ultimately successful, effort to revise the Test Act that had hitherto tended to exclude Quakers from full participation in state government. (Van Doren 1938, 314, 533–38, 550, 755).

Thomas Fitzsimmons, Pennsylvania, was another near neighbor and associate in the life of Philadelphia. An enthusiastic, Irish-born, highly successful American patriot, Fitzsimmons contributed five thousand pounds to help support the Continental Army.

Elbridge Gerry, Massachusetts, an experienced Boston merchant and politician, had served with Franklin in the Continental Congress of 1776 and signed the Declaration of Independence. An unregenerate foe of the constitution and, later, of its ratification, Gerry still felt sure enough of Franklin's personal friendship to offer a visiting constituent the honor of calling on Franklin at his home.

Jared Ingersoll, Pennsylvania, was the son of a British colonial officer in Connecticut. Father and son, bearing the same names, had both met and corresponded with Franklin for more than twenty years. The son studied law at the Middle Temple while Franklin was in London as spokesman for the Pennsylvania Assembly. The father was also in London as a Connecticut agent; he and Franklin appeared together before Prime Minister George Grenville on the Stamp Tax Act of 1765.

William Samuel Johnson, Connecticut, was the son of Samuel Johnson, first President of King's College. Franklin probably first met the twenty-three-year-old son in 1750 when he visited Stamford, Connecticut, and then invited the father to direct the English section of the proposed Pennsylvania Academy. The elder Johnson, however, declined the invitation. The younger Johnson also doubtless knew Franklin in London when from 1767 to 1771 he was a Connecticut agent there.

John Langdon, New Hampshire, served briefly with Franklin in the Continental Congress of 1775–76. Later he became congressional agent for captured British vessels.

William Livingston, New Jersey, was a member of the Continental Congress of 1775–76. He left in June to take command of the state militia while his brother, Philip, remained to sign the Declaration of Independence.

Thomas Mifflin, Pennsylvania, a devoted supporter of the revolution, had served in the near-impossible role of quartermaster-general in the Continental Army. A Quaker, he was expelled from that faith because of his military service. He visited Europe briefly in 1764; very likely he called on Franklin who was then in London.

Gouverneur Morris, Pennsylvania, had been one of the youngest and most brilliant members of the Continental Congress, representing his native state, New York. In that capacity, he drafted instructions for Franklin in Paris for both the Treaty of Alliance with France and the Treaty of Peace with Britain.

Robert Morris, Pennsylvania, an active member of the Continental Congress and of the Committee on Safety and a signer of the Declaration of Independence. Before Franklin left for Paris the two men completed arrangements (about which even the Congress was not informed) to transfer a large shipment of arms and ammunition from France to the Continental Army via a port in the West Indies. Later, as the Superintendent of Finance, Robert Morris with the help of Gouverneur Morris (not related) and the cooperation of Franklin in Paris, managed to finance the decisive campaign at Yorktown. He did this through accounting and purchasing procedures, by prodding the states for contributions, and with French loans.

George Read, Delaware, although born in Maryland, had been a member of the Continental Congresses of 1775 and 1776 and a somewhat reluctant signer of the Declaration of Independence.

John Rutledge, South Carolina, had been a member of the 1775 Continental Congress at the same time as Franklin. John's brother, Edward, a member of the 1776 Congress, had signed the Declaration of Independence and later journeyed with Franklin and John Adams to Staten Island where they consulted Lord Howe in a last, forlorn, doomed effort to avert war with Britain.

Roger Sherman, Connecticut, was Franklin's colleague in the Continental Congress of 1775 and 1776. He served with Franklin on several important congressional committees, including the Drafting Committee which, with Jefferson as chief penman, prepared the Declaration of Independence.

George Washington, Virginia, among all the convention delegates, was Franklin's acquaintance of longest standing. They had worked together under varied circumstances over many years. Both were active in the Masonic order. Both were involved in General Braddock's ill-fated campaign in 1755. The next year they had planned a joint effort by Virginia and Pennsylvania to connect Winchester and Philadelphia by road. Both were members of the Continental Congress of 1775 until Washington left Philadelphia to organize the American forces. In 1776, before leaving for Paris, Franklin conferred with Washington in Cambridge about the support requirements for the Continental Army (Van Doren 1938, 228, 261, 526).

Hugh Williamson, North Carolina, born in Pennsylvania in 1735, studied for a time at the College of Philadelphia, taking a degree in 1757. Since Franklin was a life-time trustee of that small institution and the devoted president of its board from 1749 to 1756, it seems very likely that Franklin became acquainted with young Williamson at that time. By 1774 the two men were in close touch in London. Williamson gave Franklin the Hutchinson papers that created political turmoil in both America and England. He moved to North Carolina in 1777 (Ferris and Carleton 1986, 219; Van Doren, 1938, 444ff).

James Wilson, Pennsylvania, had served in the Continental Congress of 1776, he and Franklin being on a committee of three (with Patrick Henry) to deal with the Indian tribes west of Pennsylvania and Virginia. Wilson and Franklin stood together in the Pennsylvania delegation to adopt the Declaration of Independence. Wilson was a member of a committee of seven, Franklin and Robert Morris being the other Pennsylvania members, to draft treaties of commerce and amity to be offered to European powers.

George Wythe, Virginia, met Franklin in 1776 when they were both delegates to the Continental Congress and signers of the Declaration of Independence. Wythe, with Adams and Sherman, drafted the instructions that sent Franklin and a small committee, in midwinter, on a dangerous, toilsome, and hopeless mission to Canada seeking help in the revolution.

In addition to these fairly well-established friends, Franklin must have been known, by reputation at least, to most of the other arriving delegates.

AGE, OUTLOOK, PARTICIPATION

At eighty-one, Franklin was by far the oldest delegate, as indeed he had been by far the senior member of the Continental Congress. He had been advocating a united America for a very long time. He had argued powerfully, if not effectively, for colonial unity when Madison was only a child of three years. The youngest delegate at the Constitutional Convention was Jonathon Dayton, twenty-six, of New Jersey. Franklin had a *grandson* older than that! The average age of the framers was forty-three. Franklin was thus thirty-eight years older than the average delegate. Even the second oldest delegate, Roger Sherman of Connecticut, was only sixty-six, Franklin's junior by a good fifteen years.

Jefferson, from his post in Paris, declared that Philadelphia was host to "an assembly of demigods." His estimate was based on his knowledge of what the members had already accomplished. No less than thirty-nine delegates were past or present members of the Continental Congress and so, of course, were known to Jefferson. Had the Sage of Monticello, in addition, tried to predict their futures, he might have been, if possible, even more extravagant in his praise.

The Convention included five future Supreme Court justices (Blair, Ellsworth, Paterson, Rutledge, Wilson), two future presidents (Washington, Madison), one future vice president (Gerry), four future cabinet members (Hamilton, McHenry, Madison, Randolph), fourteen future Members of the House of Representatives, nine future U.S. Senators, and twelve state governors. This small group of men, plus Adams and Jefferson, provided the effective leadership of the United States government well into the nineteenth century.

Delegates differed greatly in the extent of their participation in the Convention. Wilson and Gouverneur Morris, both from Pennsylvania, are recorded as speakers more often than any other delegate (170 and 168 times). Thus, neither Franklin nor any other Pennsylvanian needed to seek the chairman's eye to ensure that Pennsylvania's viewpoint was registered. Franklin himself spoke only thirty-one times, always quite briefly, as was his lifelong custom, but with eloquence, persuasiveness, and, usually, with substantial effect.

For Franklin, the convention, as he must have realized, was his last hurrah. In public service the old man had much to recall with pride but, at his age, little to expect with hope. Such a concerned detachment, actuated by a brilliant mind and immense gifts of expression, could make the oldest man at the meeting a uniquely valuable participant—even in "an assembly of demigods."

3

Vexatious Delays

CONVENTION CHARACTERISTICS

To estimate, as completely and as closely as possible, the nature and scope of Franklin's role in the Constitutional Convention one needs to venture somewhat beyond the records of his speeches. Thanks to the industry and foresight of James Madison, we can learn, albeit incompletely, what Franklin and other delegates said on the convention floor. Neither Madison nor any other chronicler, unfortunately, has left a comparable record of Franklin's informal conversations. Absent such records, an alternative approach is to study the conduct of the convention itself, considering how Franklin's known viewpoints and previous experiences would affect his behavior.

Several characteristics of the convention will be thus examined in this and successive chapters:

1. Delegates were impeded and annoyed by competing responsibilities, late arrivals, early departures, and frequent changes in attendance. (Chapter 3)

2. The Convention often considered the supposed wishes and opinions of constituents, about which in many cases delegates were ignorant or badly informed. (Chapter 4)

3. Debates frequently involved some very long speeches; a few delegates spoke often, early, and late on nearly every issue; others said little or nothing on any issue. (Chapter 5)

4. The record reveals many examples of anger, ignited by controversy, and exploded in thinly disguised hostility. (Chapter 6)

5. The Convention sensed the historic, enduring, and worldwide importance of its work as well as the probable penalties for failure. (Chapter 7)

PREAMBLE TO PHILADELPHIA

In March 1787, President Benjamin Franklin was pleased to hear that the Continental Congress had just designated Philadelphia as the site for a Constitutional Convention to meet in only two months. This location would require some extra effort from the distinguished President of Pennsylvania who had recently observed his eighty-first birthday. But, really, where else could the Congress reasonably locate such a momentous assembly?

Philadelphia was the well-remembered site of the Declaration of Independence. The Continental Congress met there from 1774 to 1782, except during the British military occupation of the city in the 1777–78 winter. Although the Congress had assembled in several other places since then, and was currently meeting in New York, Philadelphia leaders looked forward with some confidence to reclaiming its distinction as the seat of any new government that might be formed.

The warm-up session on interstate cooperation, held in Annapolis in September, 1786, had not been a great success. Only five states had sent delegations to the little county-seat port. Even the host state, Maryland, had failed to provide a delegation. The dozen delegates included James Madison and Alexander Hamilton. The latter drafted the only important document of the meeting, a resolution to try again in about eight months in Philadelphia. Franklin, very recently returned after nine years as American representative in Paris, did not undertake the arduous journey to Annapolis. It was just as well; the meeting had adjourned indecisively after only three days.

AWAITING A QUORUM

In Philadelphia, irritations among the delegates set in even before the convention could hold its first session. On 14 May, the date officially fixed by the Continental Congress for the opening session, only the Pennsylvanians and one other delegation (Virginia) were on hand. This was not an unusual difficulty; the Continental Congress itself was often unable to muster a quorum—even to transact urgent business. The competition of other responsibilities and interests, the immense difficulties of travel, the long distances, bad weather, and the leisurely habits of most men of property were not conducive to promptness. There was no recourse except to wait for more delegations to arrive.

After the first week of waiting, Washington wrote Arthur Lee that the delays "sour the tempers of the punctual Members who do not like to idle away their time." Madison, writing to Jefferson on 15 May, complained vaguely about the slow start. To his father, Madison was more explicit. The waiting period, he said bluntly, was "a daily disappointment." George Read wrote on 21 May, "The gentlemen who came here early . . . express much uneasiness at the backwardness of individuals in giving attendance."

In the clear, cold light of hindsight, one can see now that, although the delays in starting the sessions were irksome, they turned out to be well-disguised blessings. Punctuality at conferences, then as now, was the thief of time. However, the repeated delays gave the Pennsylvania and Virginia delegations time to prepare carefully and to devise a strategy. Then, as now, delegates well-prepared were most likely to succeed. During a full week, perhaps longer, the Virginia delegation met each morning and, in the afternoon, joined the Pennsylvania delegates for informal talks. There Franklin, eighty-one, "the Sage of the Convention," met Madison, thirty-six, "the Father of the Constitution" (Farrand 1966, 3:183).

Another disguised advantage of the delay arose from those informal sessions. Some members of the Pennsylvania delegation, notably the two unrelated Morrises, Robert and Gouverneur, urged that Virginia and Pennsylvania agree in advance to deny the small states the traditional equal vote in the coming convention. The one-state-one-vote formula was, by then, well established in the rules and customs of the Continental Congress. Still, the Pennsylvanians cautiously suggested, this unreasonable regulation could be firmly set aside for the important Philadelphia meeting. The Virginians, however, "discountenanced and stifled" that suggestion. Their good reasons, as later recalled and recorded by Madison, were that such attempts might create altercations fatal to the purposes of the meeting. All concluded, at last, that it would be wiser to urge the small states "to give up their equality for the sake of an effective government" than to invite them to "disarm themselves" at the outset of the convention.

The uncertainty about whether or when the convention could begin was ended by a completed quorum on 25 May. That source of vexation was replaced at once by two others: by frequent changes in the daily attendance, and by fruitless but inevitable speculations about when the delegates might complete their work and return home.

ARRIVING LATE, LEAVING EARLY

If some good incidental results flowed from the delay in assembling a quorum, no helpful influence at all can be ascribed to the ceaseless ebb and flow of delegates into the meeting and out of it.

Even after a quorum arrived and the meeting was ceremoniously opened, the record of delegates in "giving attendance" remained imperfect.

Late arrivals and early departures created daily changes in attendance for each of the five sessions in May and for about 40 percent of the sessions through June, July, and August.

Rhode Island ignored the request of the Continental Congress and sent no delegates at all. This boycott created bitter resentment. Washington, for example, fumed that Rhode Island's studied indifference was "impolitic, unjust, and scandalous." Delegates vented their anger by referring to the recalcitrant state as "Rogue Island" (Peters 1987, 12).

The two delegates from New Hampshire reached Philadelphia on 23 July when the convention was almost half over. Maryland did not even name its delegates until two weeks after the scheduled date of the opening session. The chief Maryland spokesman, Attorney General Luther Martin, did not reach Philadelphia for another two weeks after he was formally designated.

Pierce Butler of South Carolina tried, by motion, to minimize the anticipated difficulties by proposing that the rules "provide against the interruption of business by absence of members." His proposal was referred to the Rules Committee, which the next day reported a carefully guarded rule that "no member be absent from the House *so as to interrupt the representation of the State, without leave*" (emphasis added; Madison 1966, 27). This rule, it appears, was approved without objection or debate, but there is no record of any attempt to enforce it. Indeed, it is difficult to imagine any practical means to enfoce such a rule, either as adopted or as originally proposed by Butler.

There were, in fact, numerous instances of early departures and extended absences. James McHenry, a delegate from Maryland, left the convention as the first week ended and stayed away from the city for all of June, all of July, and the first week of August. Two New York delegates left the convention on 10 July and did not return at all. William Pierce of Georgia left Philadelphia on Sunday 1 July to take up his duties as a member of the Continental Congress. Judge Oliver Ellsworth, one of the most respected architects of compromise in the convention, left on 3 August, about six weeks before adjournment.

Of the twenty-nine delegates in place for the opening session, only seventeen were still there to sign the Constitution on the closing day.[1] The difficulty of conducting a continuing debate without excessive repetition must have been augmented by these shifting tides of delegates.

One of the first to leave—and one of the most sorely missed— was George Wythe, distinguished Virginian, law professor at William and Mary, and a former teacher of Thomas Jefferson. On the opening day Wythe was appropriately elected chairman of the Committee on Rules. After only seven days, however, Wythe went home to stay when word came of the terminal illness of his wife.

The last arrival, ten weeks late, was John Francis Mercer of Maryland. This newcomer promptly addressed the convention on a wide range of topics, gave his opinions freely on several issues already discussed, assailed the political integrity of Virginians in general, and snarled that "the aristocrats would never let the President share in their plunder of the common people." Only two years before the convention, Mercer had moved to Maryland to occupy an estate that his wife had inherited. He was Virginia-born, a member of an established Virginia family, a graduate of William and Mary College at Williamsburg, a cousin and ward of George Mason, a student of law under Thomas Jefferson. This solid Virginia background makes his bitter denunciation of Virginia and its political leaders peculiarly incongruous and inexplicable (Historians 1987, 116).

Daniel Carroll, his fellow delegate from Maryland, later accused Mercer of circulating reports that French agents had infiltrated the convention and of carrying a list of twenty delegates said to be conspiring to establish a monarchy. These and other accounts of Mercer's activity in Philadelphia led J. B. Cutting[2] to inform Thomas Jefferson in Paris that he "blushed in his own bed-chamber" to hear about them.

On 29 June Mercer had applied for an advance to finance his expenses at the Philadelphia convention. The Maryland governor replied that no money had been appropriated for this purpose but Mercer, a member of the Continental Congress, insisted that in other states such advances were usual. He regretted "on an occasion of this moment" that his "private circumstances" did not permit him to use his own resources. "Without assurance of a speedy restitution of expenses to the amount of the allowance the State has affixed," Mercer told the governor, he would be unable to attend (Farrand 1966, 4:67). Evidently either Mercer or the governor found a way to deal with his expenses.[3]

Mercer provides an example of a delegate whose brief attendance did nothing to increase the effectiveness of the convention. Jefferson, who had tried to work with Mercer in other conferences, once described him as "verbose, vain, ambitious, and intriguing, . . . afflicted with a morbid sense of rage," a man who "heard with impatience any logic which was not his own." The convention was probably assisted equally by his late arrival and his early departure a week later. When he left Philadelphia, Mercer departed for good—in both senses of that phrase.

WHEN WILL IT END?

Leaving aside the ever-present possibility that the convention might break up in furious discord, the calculation of how long deliberations would continue was a recurring concern of most delegates. Thus, only two weeks after the convention began, Richard Spaight wrote to North Carolina's governor that the time required to finish the business was "entirely uncertain." All four of the North Carolina delegates then sent Caswell a joint plea, adding that, "Several members of the Convention have their wives here and other Gentlemen have sent for theirs. This seems to promise a Summer's Campaign." They again requested advances for two months' pay, reported that North Carolina currency was subject to a "considerable" discount in Pennsylvania, promised an accounting if early adjournment were taken, and applied more pressure by suggesting it would be better for them to repay a small sum than to be obliged to return, "the public service unfinished," because of a lack of funds.

A few days after the opening session, George Mason wrote home that it was impossible to estimate how long the convention would continue, "but from present appearances until July, if not later." Gloomy as the prospect then was, Mason's forecast was, it turned out, wildly optimistic (Miller 1975, 235).

On 8 July Williamson of North Carolina cautiously predicted the end of the Convention by mid-August. However, two weeks later he revised his estimate to "sometime in September." His colleague, Alexander Martin, gloomily estimated "not before September, if then."

On 15 August, Washington, using Commodore John Paul Jones as his delivery agent, wrote Lafayette that the convention would end about September 1. Less hopeful delegates meanwhile were predicting adjournment several weeks later than that. Two weeks later, even Washington was saying that adjournment would occur in October.

As early as mid-June Pierce told William Blount that the Convention "will not rise before the middle of October."

At last the delegates, increasingly impatient of further delays, managed to adjourn on 17 September 1787.

* * *

FRANKLIN AT HOME

Old Dr. Franklin was fortunately situated, removed from the impact of delays and uncertainties. He had no farm clamoring for his attention, no law offices with impatient clients, no make-or-break business deals to settle. No close relatives demanded any substantial part of his mental and spiritual resources. His home was a few yards from the meeting hall. He need not set aside time, or expend energy, to fret about when the convention would either commence or conclude its labors.

Had the convention been held in New York or some other city, it is unlikely that Franklin would have attended. Fond as he was of good company and political discussions, he would have been, at this stage in his life, even more fond of those home comforts that for so many years he had been denied. As he once told a friend, "Whatever robs an old Man of his Sleep, soon demolishes him" (Aldridge 1965, 247).

In his nearby home, off High Street (the modern Market Street) just below Fourth, Franklin had at hand his library of some 4,000 volumes, probably the best private collection of books on the west side of the Atlantic. It was in the only house Franklin ever owned, "a good House," he complacently remarked, "constructed to my Mind." Franklin and his late wife, Deborah, had planned, built, and equipped the place, bit by bit, beginning in 1765. They furnished it elegantly with porcelain, silver, and crystal. Since his return from Paris in 1785, Franklin's daughter, Mrs. Sarah Bache, was his diligent housekeeper and hostess.

His handsome dining room on the ground floor provided ample space where he could have food and refreshments served to his fellow delegates and other friends. As president (one would say governor today) of Pennsylvania, he bore congenial responsibility to entertain distinguished visitors to its capital city.

Beside his house he had a little yard, with gravel walks beween plots of grass and flowering shrubs, all in the shade of a mulberry tree. He indulged the fantasy of supposing the tree might be the forerunner of an American silk industry, elegantly and profitably clothing his fellow citizens in silk as (so he thought) the multitudinous Chinese were clad. His outdoor sitting room was a cool and pleasant meeting place on summer afternoons and evenings. "I enjoy here" he exulted, "everything that a reasonable Mind can desire."

As a veteran of important structured and informal conferences in London, Paris, and Montreal, in Albany and Carlisle, at Cambridge and Staten Island, Franklin had been required to learn to be an effective delegate despite remote locations and makeshift circumstances. In Philadelphia, on his own home field, he could use his resources to create and enjoy the friendly, if not always cooperative, personal relationships on which, like most other meetings, the Constitutional Convention in part depended.

4

The People Will Never . . .

During the deliberations on the Constitution, one of the arguments most commonly advanced on either side of pending issues began with such words as, "The people will never agree to . . ." The emphatic "never" appears in the records with hypnotic regularity.

Rather early in its work (12 June) the convention agreed by a vote of six states to three states to propose that the new Constitution be ratified by state conventions "expressly chosen by the people" rather than by the existing state legislatures.

This decision might have made the delegates less dogmatic in their predictions about the public reaction. In fact, however, the unknown and unknowable composition of the "expressly-chosen" state conventions seems to have exerted no restraining influence whatever. The delegates' predictions, and their sense of infallibility in making them, remained peremptory, unassailable, and inaccurate. As Franklin observed in another connection: "History is full of the errors of Princes."

Today, politicians and other observers often employ sampling, public opinion polls, and rapid communication to predict how the electorate, or any segment of it, will vote on recommendations and issues. In 1787 communications were slow and opinion polls unknown, but political leaders also made bold estimates of expected public reactions and promulgated their forecasts with great emphasis and complete assurance. A few illustrations follow.

WILSON AND THE EXECUTIVE

When the convention was beginning its second week, the astute James Wilson of Pennsylvania joined the debate on whether the executive office should be filled by one person or by several. He had listened with growing impatience to the well-worn argument that people would reject the single executive because they would

44

not distinguish between an elected president and a king. But, objected Wilson, "I see no evidence of the alleged antipathy of the people." Everybody knows, he added scornfully, his weak eyes flashing behind thick glasses, "that a single magistrate is not a King." To assume that people want several equal executives is to assume, said Wilson, that they want "nothing but uncontrolled, continued, and violent animosities" that would "diffuse their poison" through every aspect of public life (Madison 1966, 4 June, 49).

BUTLER AND FEDERAL COURTS

The next day, when Wilson and Madison jointly moved to empower Congress to establish lower federal courts, Pierce Butler of South Carolina declared, "*The people will not* bear such innovations; the states will revolt at such encroachments." Butler picked up support from Connecticut but the proposal was approved 8-2, with New York divided and so not counted (Madison 1966, 73). Thus, on only eight words in the Constitution, empowering Congress "to constitute tribunals inferior to the Supreme Court," rests the whole present panoply of the United States judiciary. Contrary to Butler's fears, the people have generally, and without "revolt," accepted the U.S. District Courts, Tax Courts, Customs Courts, Patent Courts, Appeals Courts, and an array of United States Commissioners, Referees, Judges, and court employees.

PATERSON AND REPRESENTATION

When discussion began on Randolph's proposal that each state's representation in Congress be proportionate to its free population or to its wealth, Paterson of New Jersey said that delegates who supported that formula would be charged with "usurpation" by their constituents. The American people, he warned, are "sharp-sighted and not to be deceived." They are "not ripe," he added, for any step "beyond the Federal scheme" that provided equal votes for each state. "The people will not follow us," he concluded flatly, leaving the strong inference that Randolph's proposal was a waste of time (Madison 1966, 9 June, 95).

Later that day, more angry words from Paterson. He had detected, in earlier remarks by Wilson of Pennsylvania, a threat that the large states might confederate "among themselves" if the small states refused to concur. "Let them unite if they please" Paterson warned, "but let them remember that they have no authority to compel the others to unite." New Jersey, he insisted, "will *never* confederate" on this plan. He himself would "rather submit to a Monarch, to a despot, than to such a fate."[1]

As late as 16 June Paterson was still insisting, "I came here not to speak my own sentiments but the sentiments of those who sent me" (Madison 1966, 123). Yet when a compromise developed as the convention plodded on, Paterson and the New Jersey delegation accepted it. They had secured what the delegation really wanted most, a voting power in the Senate equal to that of Pennsylvania or Virginia or any other state. Before autumn arrived the New Jersey delegation had signed the draft Constitution and, before the year 1787 was out, the state convention had voted *unanimously* to approve it. Clearly, public opinion had "ripened" much more rapidly than Paterson predicted, although perhaps not more rapidly than he really expected.

GERRY AND CONGRESSIONAL TERMS

When the Convention considered the tenure of House members, a term of three years was at first suggested. Gerry of Massachusetts expansively and explosively reacted, not just for his own state but for his entire region. "The people of *New England*," he began, "will *never* give up the point of annual elections . . . the only defense of the people against tyranny." He was as much opposed, he cried, to triennial elections as he would be to a hereditary president.

This studied implication that a three-year term for elected legislators was equivalent to installing a monarchy brought Madison to his feet in rebuttal. If popular opinion is to guide us, he began, it will be difficult to fix our course. "We ought to consider what is right and necessary in itself." If that is done, "all the most enlightened and respectable citizens" will support our plan. But if we propose no proper recommendation we will not only encounter the opposition of the "influential class of citizens" but also lose the support of "the unreflecting multitude." Gerry, however, refused to budge. His countenance occasionally twisted by a facial tic and his voice stammering in earnestness (Colliers and Collier 1986, 239), he repeated his odd identification of a three-year legislative term with kingly rule. Holding the support of his own delegation only with difficulty. Gerry managed also to win over Connecticut and both Carolinas. Thus, the proposal for a three-year term carried only 7-4. Much later, a compromise two-year term replaced three years (Madison 1966, 12 June, 107).

Elbridge Gerry, on another occasion, estimated that an approach towards monarchy would be supported by fewer than one citizen out of a thousand. Loyalist opposition to the revolution was far more common than that. This delegate, whose name and conduct would later put the verb "gerrymander"[2] into the American language, predicted that proposals from the convention might lose public support if they were "of such a nature as to rouse violent opposition. . . . discord and confusion will ensue, and it is even possible that we may become a prey to foreign powers." Admitting that too-frequent elections had some unfortunate results, Gerry insisted that a Senate term of more than four years, or five at the most, "*never* would be adopted by the people" (Madison 1966, 26 June, 197). However, under the Constitution, a six-year Senate term has been in effect in every state for two centuries without "violent opposition."

LANSING AND NATIONAL GOVERNMENT

Assailing the Virginia plan as a whole, Lansing of New York predicted that it would not be accepted by the states or the people. "We know," he boldly affirmed, "what the present sentiments of the people are." It is unwise, he insisted, to expect future changes in popular sentiment. The states, he said positively, will "never" have enough confidence in a national government to empower it, by a "totally novel" scheme, to set aside state law (Madison 1966, 16 June, 122).

MORRIS AND UNITY

By 5 July, Gouverneur Morris, perhaps inspired by sentiments accompanying the Independence Day recess, took a somewhat broader view of popular opinion. The views of the people, he said flatly, are unknown and unknowable. "If the plan we recommend be reasonable and right," he assured his colleagues, "all who have reasonable minds and sound intentions will embrace it. . . . This country," he concluded, "must be united. If persuasion does not unite it, the sword will." In that event, "the scenes of horror attending civil commotion can not be described . . . and the Gallows and Halter will finish the work of the Sword" (Madison 1966, 5 July, 240).

The dire predictions of popular opposition and even open revolt became less frequent as the convention wore on. Or perhaps Madison grew weary of recording them. However, some such prophesies continued through the entire session.

MARTIN AND THE MILITIA

On August 23, for example, there were two instances of the "never" forecast. The convention considered the circumstances under which the national government would control the militia. Luther Martin of Maryland who "turned a phrase like a knife and clung like a bulldog" confidently predicted that "the States will never give up the power over the militia." His position, although strongly stated, was supported only by Connecticut, rejected by nine other states. The provisions of Article I, Section 8, empowering Congress to call up the militia, now apply to Maryland, Connecticut, and forty-eight states (Madison 1966, 515, 23 August).

RUTLEDGE AND CONGRESSIONAL POWER

Later that day, the convention had before it a proposal to empower Congress, by a two-thirds vote of both houses, to veto laws enacted by a state legislature. John Rutledge of South Carolina put his strenuous opposition in a rhetorical question: "Will any State ever agree to be bound hand and foot in this manner?" He called the proposal (which had been made by his fellow delegate, Charles Pinckney), "this shackle" and said hotly that its adoption "would damn and ought to damn the Constitution." A move to refer Pinckney's proposal to a committee was defeated and at last young Dr. Pinckney (Princeton, LL.D., April 1787) withdrew his proposal (Madison 1966, 23 August, 518–19).

WASHINGTON RAISES A STANDARD

The many predictions of popular hostility to various provisions of the constitution must have been very disturbing to the convention's President, George Washington. His words, as recalled much later by Gouverneur Morris in the Funeral Oration, and since quoted on many a monument and in many a textbook, provide a convenient summary of this aspect of a prolonged debate:

> If to please the people we offer what we ourselves disapprove, how can we afterwards defend our work? Let us raise a standard to which the wise and the honest can repair. The event is in the hand of God (Farrand 1966, 3:382, Dec. 31, 1799).

* * *

FRANKLIN AND PUBLIC OPINION

In the Convention, Franklin's record suggests no deep interest in the repeated attempts of others to predict and proclaim public opinion about the issues that emerged from it.

Franklin avoided predicting that the people of Pennsylvania, or the people of any other region, would reject the Constitution. Nor did he predict that people would approve it. He did not support his own proposals by predicting that public reaction to them would be violent, rash, calm, enthusiastic, or indifferent. He had too much respect for public opinion to guess at its content or to use the prediction as a weapon to enlist support from other delegates.

He would certainly extend more respect to public opinion itself than to efforts to calculate and declare it in advance.

Many examples throughout his long life confirm that Franklin listened to public opinion and felt a duty to try to influence it by persuasion and reason. Witness his almost uncountable published letters and polemic pamphlets.

On the other hand, Franklin had learned by experience that a rational view of one's interest is not always an effective stimulus to action. He learned this lesson when the colonies would not cooperate without an act of Parliament and when all concerned parties failed to implement his Albany Plan of unity.

Franklin clearly believed and said that popular opposition to a public measure is no proof of its impropriety—even if the opposition be fomented by powerful and distinguished leaders. Nor, of course, would he have considered public endorsement proof of the wisdom of all proposed legislation. He had spent too many years watching the British Parliament to believe that the "voice of the people" as uttered by that body was conclusive proof of divine approbation. He well knew that other Parliaments, as much as that of the British, could be led by selfish and improvident minds to resist rational and wholesome advice. He held, as did Madison and Washington, that public opinion alone should not completely control enduring constitutional principles. He must have been aware that delegates could not say with so much assurance what their constituents believed, much less what they would think if they possessed the convention's information and experience, still less what they would believe six months or a year later.

Franklin, in the Convention Hall and in informal discussions, urged his colleagues to speak up and to propose what they believed practical, right, and necessary. Nevertheless, he accepted popular opinion as the final source of governmental policy.

5
Words, Words . . .

Repetition of the same old arguments, even if they were sometimes spiced by eloquence, must have been a sore trial to irritable
and impatient delegates. Although late comers may have been
briefed by their state colleagues on what had happened before
their arrival, some repetition was also inevitable, particularly during the first weeks of the convention.

Repetition was fostered also by two convention procedures. The
well-established routine of thrashing out controversial items in
Committees of the Whole was supposed to expedite the plenary
sessions. In practice, delegates who had argued and lost their case
in committee often raised substantially the same issue a few days
or weeks later in the convention.

A further iterative procedure was encouraged by the rules
adopted on May 29. They allowed extensive reconsideration of
decisions already reached. Any adopted motion could be recon-
sidered, if no one objected, on the same day. Even if the motion to
reconsider provoked an objection, it could still be offered and
again debated on a single day's notice.

To the repetitions thus encouraged by convention rules and
assured by the shifting attendance, verbosity was added by human
nature. Several of the Founding Fathers contrived to confirm Poor
Richard's definition of an oration: "A Flood of Words and one
Drop of Reason."

LUTHER MARTIN

Every conference, now as then, seems sure to have at least one
delegate who talks too much. Luther Martin, attorney general of
Maryland, easily won the prolixity prize at Philadelphia. Uncouth
and untidy though he was, Martin was a brilliant attorney. He had
graduated at the head of his 1766 Princeton class. Rumbling and
colloquial, "enveloped in the sour-sweet smell of good Maryland

51

rye" (Smith 1956, 227), he seemed determined to talk long enough to recapture the time he had lost by arriving in Philadelphia two weeks late. He had only a few things to say and was willing, even anxious, to spend hours in saying them. On 27 June he held the floor for three continuous hours. Madison, although a glutton for punishment, gave up the unequal struggle for once and recorded only a resume, "the substance of a speech." Even in this digest Madison managed to inform an attentive reader how dull and how very long it all was.

Martin set out to prove "that individuals in a state of nature, and states (until they surrender their equal sovereignty) are equally free and independent." Proof of this abstruse theorem included the reading and expounding by Martin of several passages from *Two Treatises of Government* by the English physician and political philosopher, John Locke; from the essays of the English clergyman and chemist, Joseph Priestley; from a seventeenth-century principal of St. Mary's College of Glasgow University, Samuel Rutherford; from Baron Somers, the British statesman largely responsible for the 1707 Act of Union that amalgamated England and Scotland; and from the *Law of Nations* by the Swiss jurist Emerich de Vattel.

To conclude this array of scholarship for the day, Martin told the convention that he "was too much exhausted to finish his remarks" but promised to resume them the next day.

On 28 June, as promised (or threatened), Martin began again. And again Madison wrote down "the substance of the residue," adding that Martin's discourse "was delivered with much diffuseness and considerable vehemence." Robert Yates, who differed from Madison on almost every substantial point, nevertheless used almost identical language to describe the numbing effect of Martin's discourse. And Alexander Hamilton, speaking in rebuttal two days later (Yates 1987, 186), said tartly that Martin had been "at great pains to establish positions which are not denied."

Later that day Franklin suggested that prayers be offered "imploring the assistance of Heaven." Remembering Franklin's impish tendencies, one is tempted to wonder momentarily whether his appeal for supernatural assistance was offered tongue-in-cheek as a reaction to Martin's verbal onslaught.

On 14 July, speaking for the third time that eventless day, Martin declared ironically, "The states that please to call themselves 'large' are the weakest in the Union." He would prefer two confederations rather than give up equal representation.

Wilson said he was not surprised by Martin's remarks. Those who say that "a minority is more than a majority" are capable also of finding that "a minority is stronger than a majority." "I suppose," Wilson added, "the next assertion will be that small states are richer." But, he continued with ponderous sarcasm, he did not expect that their claim to greater wealth would continue after the small states were assessed for an equal share of troops or taxes (Madison 1966, 14 July, 290–91).

William Pierce of Georgia, who wrote brief sketches of his colleagues, recorded this impression of Martin: "This gentleman possesses a good deal of information but he has a very bad delivery, and is so extremely prolix that he never speaks without tiring the patience of all" (Farrand 1966, 3:93). Henry Adams has described this complex man as "drunken-generous, slovenly-grand, and reprobate-genius" (quoted by Recove in *Wilson*, 106).

ALEXANDER HAMILTON

Of course Luther Martin was not the only delegate who, in the opinion of some of his colleagues, talked too long or too often. Alexander Hamilton on 18 June, for example, held the floor for nearly a full day without interruption or respite. His remarks contained an extensive review and close comparison of the plans proposed by the Virginia and New Jersey delegations. Hamilton demonstrated theoretically the precarious nature of all confederations, validating his conclusion by historical examples. He began in the fourth century, B.C., with the Amphictyonic League of the Greek city-states, continuing through the military exploits of Philip of Macedonia in the Phoenician War, grandly but attentively sweeping on past the election of Roman emperors by the legions, and concluding with a broad survey of the organizing principles of Charlemagne, the rulers of Russia, the Swiss cantons, and the Dutch and German confederations. He finished by reading and explaining a list of eleven principles that he believed applicable to the preceding debate, commented on each principle, and vowed to raise these eleven issues "in the proper stages of future discussions" (Madison 1966, 130–39, 18 June).

EDMUND RANDOLPH

The record also shows that Governor Edmund Randolph, at the outset of the convention, spoke for the major part of a day to propose and explain the thirteen Virginia resolutions (Madison 1966, 28–33). Robert Yates of New York noted in his diary that Randolph gave "a long and elaborate speech." These opinions about the length and complexity of Randolph's speech are not surprising. Yates invariably opposed any step that might produce a stronger central government. As William Pierce of Georgia noted about Yates, "his enemies say he is an anti-federal man."

Pierce found other delegates to criticize for their excessive talk and other forensic sins. Of William Houstoun, a heavy-set and highly visible delegate from Georgia, Pierce wrote sharply that Nature had "done more for his corporeal than for his mental powers." Although granting that Houstoun had an "amiable" temper and honorable principles, Pierce also felt obliged to record that in debate the Georgian was "confused and irregular." As for Read of Delaware, Pierce found his remarks "tiresome to the last degree."

ELBRIDGE GERRY

Nor did Pierce care much for the style of Elbridge Gerry of Massachusetts. This New England merchant who, under the terms of the Constitution he roundly condemned, nevertheless would later seek and win a seat in the Congress and a position as Madison's vice president, was described by Pierce as "a laborious speaker" who was only "sometimes clear." Pierce complained further that Gerry "goes extensively into all subjects, speaks on without regard to eloquence or diction."

Gerry's fellow delegate from Massachusetts, Rufus King, in February had introduced in the Congress the Resolution to summon the convention. King tried, with indifferent success, to keep a record of the meeting. Striving to make a list of Gerry's numerous, and often complex, objections, King wrote obscurely, "The Vice-President destroys the independence of the Legislature." Then, while trying to understand Gerry's argument, King suddenly wrote, "*I give up!*" and ended his notes for the day in despair (Farrand 1966, 2:635–36). King stayed on to sign the Constitution, but there must have been moments when he wondered why on earth he had ever offered a motion to call the Convention.

JAMES MADISON

Although Madison's *Notes* usually show an antiseptic impartiality and rarely describe the feelings of the speakers, he did note on 13 September, with adjournment just a few days ahead, that the impatience of members was at last great enough to curtail debate. "A number of members being very impatient and calling for the question," Washington responded to the convention's mood by a prompt roll call on a pending amendment.

Madison noticed the "tedious and reiterated discussions" in convention, but he generally kept to his self-imposed task of recording as much as possible. Writing from New York to Jefferson in Paris a month after the convention adjourned, Madison reported that the meeting "was more difficult than can be well conceived by those who were not concerned in the execution of it." Considering how tough were the convention's problems and how talkative were its members, Madison wondered that they could agree at all. Thus the final concensus seemed to Madison "a miracle."

Hamilton, addressing the New York ratification assembly, also gave a round-by-round account of some of the wordy controversies at Philadelphia. Compromise, he said, was essential. To the suggestion of holding another convention, Hamilton was instantly and vigorously hostile. "Let another [convention] be called tomorrow, let them meet twenty times,—nay, twenty thousand times; they will have the same difficulties . . . the same clashing interests to reconcile" (Farrand 1966, 3:333).

*   *   *

FRANKLIN AS SPEAKER

Franklin had been active in conferences and other aspects of public life for the greater part of his long life. It seems unlikely that he would be unduly disturbed by frequent repetition, or by long, pointless speeches and vexatious delays. More than most delegates, Franklin had learned by long experience how to abide the impact of boredom and to make a virtue of necessity.

Even if he spoke rarely, Franklin welcomed a status that entitled him to take part in the debates when he wished to do so. His autobiography recalls how pleased he was in 1750 to be elected a burgess in the Pennsylvania Assembly, after serving as the assembly's silent and dutiful clerk for nearly twenty years. He did not enjoy the tedium of "sitting there to hear Debates in which as Clerk I could take no part, and which were often so unentertaining that I was induc'd to amuse myself with making magic Squares, or Circles, or anything to avoid Weariness." Consciously or otherwise, he seems to have been usually guided by his own four-word maxim, as expressed by Poor Richard, "Speak little, do much," or, slightly longer, "Well done is better than well-said."

That inquisitive historian, Jared Sparks, recording an 1830 visit to Madison, found that during the convention "Dr. Franklin seldom spoke." He often (but not invariably) wrote his speeches in advance, a simple precaution which helped to curb garrulity. Even Franklin's extemporaneous remarks were delivered, as Madison remembered for Sparks, "with great pertinacity and effect" (Farrand 1966, 3:481).

Franklin's long-time friend, Dr. Benjamin Rush of Philadelphia, noticed and recorded on 2 June 1787, that Franklin was attending the sessions punctually, that he was "even taking part in its business and deliberations," and that he exhibited "a spectacle of transcendent benevolence" (Farrand 1966, 3:33).

Even after the convention had adjourned forever, Franklin's relatively few words continued to exert influence. This lasting effect was enhanced by the fact that, unlike most of the other delegates' remarks, Franklin's best speeches were written. Nathaniel Gorham, back in Boston, recalled and relished Franklin's speech on the closing day (appendix A5). Gorham took the trouble to write a request for a copy of "that where you observe on the French 'Lady'" with the purpose (if Franklin was willing) of publishing it for distribution. Franklin complied with Gorham's request (Farrand 1966, 4:78, 80).

From Annapolis Daniel Carroll informed Franklin that the Franklin speech on representation, delivered on 11 June (appendix A2), as well as his remarks at the closing session, had been read to the Maryland House of Delegates (Farrand 1966, 4:79).

Although he feared that he had "transgressed" on Franklin's act of kindness in supplying him copies of the two papers, Carroll felt "compelled" to reveal their contents to the Maryland House. That body, he explained, had asked its delegates for information on the Philadelphia proceedings. He had attended the House session in Annapolis along with three other Maryland delegates—Martin, Jenifer, and McHenry (Mercer apparently did not attend that Maryland House meeting).

Carroll explained further that McHenry had "distinguished himself beyond the most sanguine hopes of his friends and the expectations of the adverse party." Beyond any doubt, the "adverse party" was Luther Martin.[1]

In Carroll's view, Martin misrepresented the motives of both Franklin and Washington so badly that Franklin's speeches must be read to the Maryland House. "I did it," Carroll wrote, "at the risk of yr displeasure, for the public Good" (Farrand 1966, 4:79, December 1787).

Franklin did not, at any stage of his life, regard himself an accomplished orator. People listened when Franklin spoke because he was likely to say something memorable. They treasured his witty, trenchant (and brief) comments. They quoted them (with or without credit to their origin) for the instruction and pleasure of their friends. He was one of those speakers whom listeners would rather quote than quarrel with. Some people, no doubt, sometimes disagreed with him, but no instance comes to mind that any listener complained of being bored by Franklin's discourse. He listened well and spoke little and his auditors enjoyed communion with a first-class intellect.

6
Controversy

Washington, writing to Hamilton in July, wished he had avoided the convention, found the clash of opinions "alarming," and rather pathetically told the younger officer, his aide-de-camp during four years of war: "I am sorry you went away. I wish you were back" (Farrand 1966, 3:36).

Washington's concern may not have been so forcefully expressed to other delegates, but the framers did confront, debate, and decide a wide range of highly controversial issues. In a typical day a dozen roll call votes might be recorded. About six hundred such votes were taken during the convention and few of them were unanimous.

Madison's day-by-day *Notes* and the fragmentary records kept by other delegates reveal, through the veil of parliamentary courtesy, sharp rivalries and profound animosities. To view the convention as a scene of urbane and dispassionate exchange of lofty views on abstract issues would put the Philadelphia meeting into a Parson Weems mode.

A few examples of angry debate suggest the wide opportunity offered by the convention to Franklin's great personal talents for conciliation and diplomacy. The convention did not need additional gladiators. It needed a delegate who had learned by experience, and now fully understood, that group action is, almost always, a result of compromise.

THE EXECUTIVE, A PERVASIVE CONTROVERSY

Ninety-three decisions on the executive were recorded in Madison's *Notes*. Of these, sixty-nine decisions (74 percent of the total) were made by a divided vote. Even procedural suggestions (to postpone, to reconsider, or to commit) were often so controversial that formal debate and a recorded vote were required. Should power be assigned to one person or divided among several executives? What title should the office bear? What qualifications should be set? Who should select the executive and for what term of office? Madison wrote Jefferson that the issues in this area were more tedious than those of any other section of the Constitution.

The presidential term of office, for example, provided an almost unlimited range of choices. Proposals ranged from serving not more than six years in any twelve to rival opinions that the president should serve "during good behavior." Martin of Maryland, however, moved a presidential term of eleven years. Gerry suggested fifteen years. Rufus King outbid them all and moved for a twenty-year term. He said, perhaps sarcastically, "This is the medium life of Princes." (He meant, of course, the average *adult* life of princes.) William Davie sought a return to reality by suggesting eight years.

Wilson said all these variations were due to an erroneous assumption—that on reaching an advanced age the president would not wish to stay in office. A doge of the Venetian Republic had been elected after he was eighty. Popes, too, were elected, in many cases, at advanced ages. An American President, on the other hand, if elected to a fifteen-year term at age thirty-five must "at the age of 50 in the very prime of life" and with all the value of experience, be cast aside like a useless hulk. Lord Mansfield in Britain, Wilson added, had held his post as chief justice for thirty *more* years *after* reaching age fifty.[1]

Other suggestions were then considered, notably Wilson's bizarre (but apparently serious) suggestion that the president be named by fifteen members of Congress who would be selected by lot and required to vote immediately so that "intrigue would be avoided." Wilson immediately added that this "was not a digested idea and might be liable to strong objections." Nevertheless after a motion to postpone was defeated, Wilson formally moved his "undigested" idea. The lean and hungry-looking Gerry said, in a rare attempt at whimsy, that such a lottery would be "committing too much to *chance*." King said, more seriously, that the country should be "governed by reason" and again suggested postponement. Wilson protested that he still thought "we ought to resort to the people for the election" and seconded the motion to postpone. This time, probably to Wilson's relief, the motion to postpone was unanimously adopted (Madison 1966, 359–62, 24 July).

Hamilton, shortly after the Philadelphia Convention had adjourned, discussed the constitutional provisions for the executive branch and offered the following remarkably accurate political prophecy to Governor Morgan Lewis, "You nor I, my friend, may not live to see the day, but most assuredly it will come, when every vital interest of the State will be merged in the all-absorbing question of *who shall be the next President?*" (Farrand 1966, 3:410).

SUSPICION FROM THE START

Although individuals and delegations varied in the openness of their belligerence, nearly all seemed profoundly suspicious about the hidden motives of the others. They were meeting in the same Philadelphia where disgruntled colonists had been eager to take on the British army. Now, only eleven years later, some delegates, although no longer colonials, seemed at times equally eager to take on one another.

Some of the letters of arriving delegates reveal their incipient hostility. On 24 May young Rufus King wrote to Jeremiah Wadsworth in Connecticut. As the convention was about to begin, King was dismayed to find himself the sole representative present from all of New England. "Pray hurry on your delegates," he urged. "It may prove most unfortunate if they do not attend within a few days." King was known as an eloquent and persuasive speaker with a firm grasp of parliamentary tactics. Nevertheless, the tone of this letter is that of a lonely scout deep in enemy territory, uncertain of the strength and battle plans of the opposition, and desperate for reinforcements.

On 3 June Wadsworth answered King's appeal with both ominous and reassuring news. The Connecticut delegates were on the way but, Wadsworth warned, Sherman of Connecticut might merely try to patch up the Articles of Confederation; he is "as cunning as the Devil, and if you attack him . . . you might as well catch an eel by the tail" (Farrand 1966, 3:26, 33).

Similarly, George Read of Delaware, urging his colleague Dickinson to hasten to join him in Philadelphia, wrote excitedly that the large states were about "to combine to swallow up the smaller ones, by addition, division, and impoverishment" (Farrand 1966, 3:26).

George Mason of Virginia, also writing home anxiously before the convention began, told his son abut "the evils which threaten us." Examining these perils Mason prayed that the convention could agree on remedies. Whether agreement was possible he was uncertain; he had already encountered what he called "some very eccentric opinions" among his fellow delegates (Farrand 1966, 3:23).

His judgment about his colleagues' opinions were disquieting enough for him to assert that he would not "upon pecuniary motives serve in the Convention for a thousand pounds a day." In short, he would serve for duty but not for love or money (Farrand 1966, 3:32).

Once the Convention was under way, suspicions became more overt. When ambitious young Charles Pinckney suggested a convention committee "to superintend the minutes," Gouverneur Morris replied that such a task was the duty of the convention secretary "as their impartial officer." A committee might distort the record "according to their opinion and wishes." Such suspicions of bias and dishonesty among delegates were just persuasive enough to defeat Pinckney's proposal, 4-5 (Madison 1966, 29 May, 28).

WALKOUT THREATS

Intense controversy arose early in serious threats to end the convention by leaving it. During the very first week George Read of Delaware threatened to depart. He held that the Delaware delegates "were restrained by their Commissions from assenting to *any* change of the rule of suffrage" [in the Congress]. In case such changes were approved in Philadelphia, Read cautioned, "it might become their duty to retire from the Convention."

Gouverneur Morris of Pennsylvania at first expressed alarm. He regretted, he said, such a proof of discord as secession by a state so early in the Convention. But, he went on firmly, the proposed change was fundamental and indispensable.

Madison followed Morris at once. He suggested "taking the sense of the members. . . ." This procedure would save the Delaware delegates embarrassment. By considering the controversial clause in Committee of the Whole, they could postpone voting. It appears possible that such parliamentary maneuvers had been orchestrated in advance by the Virginia and Pennsylvania delegations, perhaps during their meetings while awaiting the arrival of a quorum. Spontaneous or not, the devious proposal, as Madison ruefully noted, "did not appear to satisfy Mr. Read."

Madison may not have known that George Read had written his own instructions. And Read certainly didn't tell the convention. Delaware was the only state to instruct its delegates so specifically (Historians 1987, 7). In the end, its delegates accepted the compromise regardless of instructions and the little state then became the first to ratify the Constitution.

After several other delegates had argued that a Delaware secession from the convention was not really required, Read offered a motion to postpone the inflammatory question. It was adopted by common consent, the customary state-by-state roll call was omitted, and the walkout was for the time avoided. But the issue kept returning (Madison 1966, 37–38, 30 May).

On Saturday morning, 16 June, came a veiled threat by New York to leave the convention. John Lansing attacking the Virginia plan, said New York would not have participated in the convention if it had been known that the deliberations would involve "a consolidation of the states and a national government" rather than amendments to the Articles of Confederation (Madison 1966, 121–22).

William Paterson, later the same day, read out the fifth and thirteenth sections of the Articles of Confederation. The fifth section gave each State one vote; the thirteenth provided that "no alteration shall be made without unanimous consent." Continuing his history lesson, Paterson said, significantly, "this is the nature of all *treaties*" (emphasis added). The large states had readily agreed to the Articles in 1777, whereas the small states had then accepted them reluctantly (Madison 1966, 123, 16 June).

On the next convention day, Monday, 18 June, Alexander Hamilton bluntly said that no amendment that left the states in possession of complete sovereignty could possibly achieve the public safety and happiness. The state demagogues, Hamilton said scornfully, carefully calling names without naming any names, "hate the control of the general Government." State governments, he concluded, "are not necessary for any of the great purposes of commerce, revenue, or agriculture." Under both the New Jersey and the Virginia plans, the moderate wages of a member of the House of Representatives (which Hamilton once estimated at about three dollars a day) could serve as "only a bait to little demagogues" (Madison 1966, 16 and 18 June, 129–30).

BEDFORD VERSUS KING

On 30 June, chubby Gunning Bedford of Delaware gave an outspoken review of the balance of forces. All political societies, including America, he began, respond to ambition and avarice.[2] "Are we to act," he asked sarcastically, "with greater purity than the rest of mankind?" He was not intimidated, Bedford said, by the "dictatorial air" of the large states. They "dare not dissolve the Confederation. If they do, the small ones will find some foreign ally of more honor and good faith, who will take them by the hand and do them justice."

This combination of threat and candor, coming from a delegate known for his impetuous temper, evoked a bitter retort from King of Massachusetts. He had not, he insisted, used dictatorial language; "this intemperance has marked the honorable gentleman himself." Nor had he, with unprecedented vehemence, threatened to "court the protection of some foreign hand. This, too, was the language of the Honorable member himself." "I grieve," King continued mournfully, that such a thought entered Mr. Bedford's heart; even more "that such an expression had dropped from his lips." Whatever his distress, King "would never court relief from a foreign power!"

On that ringing challenge the session abruptly adjourned. Fortunately, since it was Saturday evening, the delegates had the healing hours of another Sunday to compose themselves if not to compose their differences (Madison 1966, 30 June, 229–31).

PATERSON VERSUS MORRIS

Next week, Paterson of New Jersey, by now fighting with back to wall, announced he would make no more concessions. The small states must have an equality of votes in the Senate. "My resolution is fixed. I will meet the large states on that ground and no other."

Gouverneur Morris replied virtuously that *he* had no fixed resolution except to do what was right. Equality of the States in the proposed Senate, he said, made that body only "another [Continental] Congress, a mere wisp of straw." He regretted that he had not heard any suggestions "for supporting the dignity and splendor of the American Empire." National purpose, he complained, had been constantly sacrificed to local views. Morris went on with *his* version of recent history. When the Declaration of Independence was adopted, a government had to be formed at once. "The small states . . . taking advantage of the moment, extorted from the large ones an equality of votes." Now they demand under a new system greater individual rights than their fellow citizens. "The proper answer to them is that the same necessity . . . does not now exist. The large states are at liberty now to consider what is right, rather than what may be expedient."

Morris continued with growing energy. He possessed the manners of a dandy, the reputation of a lover, a silver tongue, and a gift for the incisive phrase and the devastating allusion. He now used most of these varied talents to expound the lessons to be learned from Germany. The emperor, he said, has great prerogatives and vast resources but the nation lacks unity. Foreign powers can influence every national decision because power resides in the local authorities. It is "considered of more consequence to support the Prince of Hesse than the Happiness of the people of Germany." This was a shrewd touch; no survivor of the revolution would fail to detest the memory of King George's hated Hessian mercenaries. Do gentlemen want to follow a *German* example, Morris asked.

From bluntness Morris moved to anger. "Good God, Sir," he asked, turning to Washington in the chair, "can they so delude themselves? What if all the Charters and Constitutions of the States were thrown into the fire, and all their demagogues into the ocean? What would it be to the happiness of America?"

Roger Sherman and Oliver Ellsworth hastily moved to postpone further discussion. Even in that company of emphatic individualists, joint sponsorship of a motion by these two Connecticut Yankees must have provided a memorable experience. The ungainly, long-necked Sherman was "the oddest-shaped character I ever remember," wrote Pierce, and his strange New England dialect was "grotesque and laughable" even though "no man has a better heart or a clearer Head" (Farrand 1966, 3:88). Judge Ellsworth was known as the most avid consumer of snuff in Connecticut, perhaps in America, a robust, six-foot-two delegate who spoke out seldom but often "mumped" to himself *sotto voce* in the midst of debate (Peters 1987, 29).

The Connecticut motion squeaked through, 6-5, and Washington promptly adjourned the session for another healing weekend (Madison 1966, 7 July, 253–56).

PATERSON VERSUS RANDOLPH

Although the Committee on Compromise had on 5 July submitted a report that was ultimately adopted by the convention, the issue of representation for large and small states was still unsettled. Randolph then said that, since the opponents of the Virginia plan were unwilling even to refer the matter to a committee, the convention should adjourn. Then, he added in exasperation, the large states could consider "the steps to be taken in the present solemn crisis."

Paterson at once, and much too eagerly, agreed, adding that the secrecy rule should first be rescinded so that "our constituents" could be informed and consulted. Let Randolph formally offer a motion to adjourn *sine die;* Paterson said he would second it "with all my heart."

General Pinckney, delegate from South Carolina, immediately asked whether Randolph had meant a final adjournment or just an adjournment for the rest of the day. If the former, Pinckney simply could not now promise to repeat the long trip to and from Charleston. It is easy to sympathize with him.[3]

Randolph protested that he had "never entertained an idea of an adjournment *sine die."* He regretted that Paterson had misinterpreted his motion "so readily and so strangely." Randolph had proposed an adjournment only to permit "some conciliatory experiment" and, if the small states persisted, to let the large states "take such measures—he would not say what—as might be necessary."

Paterson then seconded the motion to adjourn until the next day. He was unable to resist adding that the large states might well use the time to think about conciliation. The motion to adjourn was put, the roll-call again produced a tie, and the discussion continued. John Rutledge, however, saw no hope for a compromise; the small states had solemnly repeated their fixed policy; the large states simply had to decide whether or not to yield.

A motion to adjourn for the day, being offered again and put again, was at last adopted, 2-7, while Georgia was divided and so not counted (Madison 1966, 16 July, 300–301).

IMPORTATION OF SLAVES

On August 25 the convention in plenary session gingerly approached a final decision on importing slaves. A committee had earlier recommended a constitutional ban on importation after the year 1800. General Pinckney moved to defer the cutoff date to 1808 and Gorham of Massachusetts (perhaps with an eye to New England commercial interest) seconded the motion. Madison objected. Another twenty years of importing, he declared, "will produce all the mischief that can be apprehended." Such a permit, he felt, would be "more dishonorable to the National character than to say nothing about it in the Constitution." Madison's objections were not effective. Virginia was joined only by Pennsylvania, New Jersey, and Delaware in the negative.

Immediately after the vote, Gourverneur Morris observed that the adopted resolution was clearly a concession to three slave-importing states. Morris therefore suggested that the text read, "importation of slaves into North Carolina, South Carolina, and Georgia shall not be prohibited. . . ." Mason said he feared such explicitness "might give offense to the people" of the three named states. Hugh Williamson of North Carolina said he was against slavery "both in opinion and practise" but thought it unwise to exclude these three states from the Union. Morris at length withdrew his motion.

Thus the text of Section 9, Article 1, of the United States Constitution, with all its freight of future sorrow, war, and inhumanity, was approved on a vote of 7-4 (Madison 1966, 25 August, 530–31).[4]

* * *

FRANKLIN AS CONCILIATOR

Franklin, more perhaps than most other delegates, felt the need for a constitution at this point in his country's development. Even before the revolution, in 1774, he wrote, "I wish most sincerely that a Constitution was formed and settled for America, that we might know what we are and what we have, what our Rights and what our Duties" (quoted in Connors 1965, 55). If he felt this strongly as a loyal colonial, he surely would be even more eager, as a leader of a newly independent nation, for an orderly and authoritative statement of rights and duties.

Like other thoughtful delegates, Franklin regarded the Philadelphia proceedings as fateful—not only for Americans but for all mankind. Failure of the convention would lead people everywhere "from this unfortunate instance to despair of establishing government by Human Wisdom and leave it to chance, war, and conquest" (McDonald 1988, 6).

The Philadelphia convention was by no means Franklin's first opportunity to share in developing a plan of government. In the private sector, as early as 1734, Franklin had arranged and published *Anderson's Constitutions* for the use of colonial members of the Masonic Order (Carter 1955, 124). More comprehensively, Franklin had created, tested, or installed the rules for managing the Philadelphia *Junto*, the fire brigade, the city watch, the College of Pennsylvania, the city hospital, the circulating library, and the American Philosophical Society. He was a community leader long before he became a political official.

In addition to such varied local and personal enterprises,

Franklin possessed extensive experience in the higher circles of government. His first rough sketch of Colonial Union had been drafted in 1751 (Van Doren 1938, 214). Franklin prepared a well-known Plan of Union at the Albany Congress in 1754. A committed nationalist and democrat, as a delegate to the Continental Congress of 1775, he prepared the first draft and moved the adoption of the "Articles of Confederation and Perpetual Union for the United Colonies of North America." The Congress, still hoping at that time for reconciliation, did not act on Franklin's motion.

In 1776 Franklin was named president of the state convention that wrote a constitution for Pennsylvania. In 1786 he was drafted to the Pennsylvania State Assembly by the almost unanimous desire of conflicting parties that he "might find some means of reconciling them," especially in the revision of the Test Act.

Thus by 1787 very few voluntary or governmental relationships were completely novel to the rich experience of Benjamin Franklin.

In the federal convention other delegates revealed in their remarks a clear, often strong, and always present belief that each of them was expected to advance and protect the interest of his State. By contrast Franklin typically exhibited no sectional prejudices. Like Washington, Franklin had served the entire country so long and so devotedly that, by habit as well as by reasoned conviction, he put the nation first, beyond local, state, or regional concerns. Pleased and proud though he was to be a citizen of Philadelphia and of Pennsylvania, Franklin argued on 11 June (appendix A2) that "it would be better if every member of Congress . . . were to consider himself rather as a representative of the whole than as an Agent for the interests of a particular State." In Philadelphia in 1787, as Franklin himself recognized, the time for that ideal had not yet come; nor has it fully arrived two centuries later.

Throughout the Convention Franklin was like a skilled cabinet-maker who "when the edges of planks do not fit . . . takes a little from both, and makes a good joint" for a broad table (appendix A4). If his first suggested compromise was unacceptable, he could propose other ideas, and he advised delegates to spend time "not in associating with their own party and devising new arguments to fortify themselves in their old opinions but . . . mix with members of opposite sentiments, lend a patient ear to their reasonings, and candidly allow them all the weight to which they may be entitled" (Farrand 1966, 3:471).

Many delegates, from both large states and small states, were clearly maneuvering to make their opponents responsible for the possible failure of the convention. Who, other than Franklin, could care about a successful agreement more than about the advantage of one state over another, or the placement of credit or blame? Franklin had not only the motive for success but also the skills and the experience to bring it to pass. He, more than any other delegate, could draw on years of diplomatic experience to invest in a successful outcome. He, more than any younger member of the Convention, could be free from the controls of expectation and ambition, free from fear that his words might be interpreted as an inadequate defense of the goals of his constituents.

Franklin had not only skill and opportunity, but also determination to persuade the delegates to "part with some of their demands, in order that they may join in some accommodating proposition" (appendix A4). In an assembly of fluent, resourceful, and quarrelsome men, of close votes and tie votes, of repeated threats to walk out, of sarcasm, stubbornness, and sulks, Franklin's tact and wit were unique—and essential.

7

Hopes and Fears

As the founders straggled into Philadelphia in May, June, and July 1787, they already could see that it would be far more difficult to create a new government than it was to declare independence. The revolution of 1776 rested on a breathtaking, but simple, eloquent, and brief declaration of intent. To give effect to that purpose, the Articles of Confederation had turned out to be inadequate. The Articles did not go into effect for five years; they were at last ratified in 1781.

The Constitution of 1787, on the other hand, required of Franklin and his colleagues not merely assent to glorious principles but also the dusty engineering of government powers, precise specifications, frank exchanges, uncertain compromises, and close decisions.

However, the convention was necessary because the colonies had been allied against a common enemy; they were not yet unified by a common loyalty. Their Articles of Confederation could be changed only by unanimous consent and any one state could prevent action by any of the other twelve, or by all of the other twelve together. Several attempts to strengthen the Congress had been thwarted by this unanimity rule.

NO FIRM LEAGUE OF FRIENDSHIP

The Continental Congress, after little more than a decade, was losing its struggle to govern America. Organized under the flags of thirteen independent republics, the former colonies were unwilling to give their Congress effective authority. Nevertheless previous sessions of this Congress felt free to borrow money anywhere, at home or abroad, and if loans were not sufficient, to print currency almost at will.

The economic results of such policies could be seen in the accounts of the national government. In 1786 the *total* income

69

available to the Continental Congress was less than one-third of the *interest* on the national debt. Although borrowing was now restricted and the printing of national currency discontinued, among the unfortunate current results of earlier practices was a national currency, as the saying went, "not worth a Continental," and an army that, even during a war for survival, was still ill-fed, ill-armed, ill-housed, ill-clad, and ill-tempered.

The Articles of Confederation described this arrangement as "a firm league of friendship." It was, in fact, neither firm nor friendly.

When Washington ordered his troops to swear loyalty to the Union, some of them refused in bewilderment. "Our Country is New Jersey," the nonconformists insisted.

When George Rogers Clark won control of the old Northwest Territory by seizing a few British forts along the Mississippi and the Wabash, his orders came from Patrick Henry, governor of Virginia.

When a rider galloped to Philadelphia to report the surrender at Yorktown, Congress did not have enough honest money in the till to pay the messenger's expenses.

When peace came, the thirteen republics engaged at once in bitter economic warfare. Civil disorders grew violent. Georgia imposed martial law. In Western Massachusetts, a movement called Shays' Rebellion organized some two thousand armed farmers to attack five county courthouses (Peters 1987, 11).

The powers of Europe meanwhile seemed to circle like vultures waiting for the confused champions of "inalienable rights" to weary of such radical concepts and be annexed to some strong orderly kingdom. The Pennsylvania militia had fired on would-be settlers from Connecticut. The British still held key forts on the Great Lakes. Spain was trying to close the Mississippi from Natchez to New Orleans, and Congress was ready to exchange its claims to the Father of Waters for a Spanish trade treaty. Vermont was considering rejoining the British Empire (that was "a sore thorn" wrote Washington). New York was taxing trade across the mouth of the Hudson between New Jersey and Connecticut (Wilson 1987, Onuf, 99–103).

The very existence of the United States was at stake. Some delegates may not have perceived a clear and present danger but to the most knowledgeable members of the convention the country seemed to be in a desultory drift to disintegration.

This conclusion is strongly supported by comparing the text of the enabling legislation with the report of the 1786 Annapolis

Convention. The Annapolis commissioners had cautiously asked for a convention "to render the Constitution of the Federal Government adequate to the exigencies of the Union." The Congress, however, extended the Annapolis recommendation. It voted for a meeting in Philadelphia "to render the Constitution adequate to the exigencies of Government *and the preservation of the Union*" (emphasis added). Congress thus admitted that it could not preserve the Union—let alone govern it or defend it.

Pelatiah Webster put the situation in a homely metaphor: "Thirteen staves and never a hoop will not make a barrel!" while Noah Webster characteristically summarized his view in one carefully-chosen word: He said the government of the Confederation was "a cobweb" (Peters 1987, 5).

PLANNING FOR AN UNKNOWN FUTURE

The Founding Fathers were trying to legislate for a country that was certain to change but did not yet exist. They tried, with indifferent success, to look into the seeds of time. They quarreled about the impact that the development of additional states would have, or should have, on the body politic. Some feared that the new states would impair the commitment and cohesiveness of the nation; others looked confidently upon the expected new states as a potential advantage.

All seem to have been impressed by the vastness of their new nation. They spoke in glowing terms of its resources, its room to grow, its opportunities. Their satisfaction in their prospects was much restrained, however, by the perils of growth and change. They were beset by nagging doubts whether their convention could find a formula to manage and guide and civilize such a growing giant. They worried about what would happen if some states, but only some, ratified their new plan of government. Suppose the parts of the new nation thus created were not contiguous? Could a series of "islands" separated by alien areas be governed and defended?

All were agreed that the Articles of Confederation under which they had tried to function for eleven years were unsatisfactory. There remained great differences of opinion about the appropriate "alternatives." Some felt that only minor changes were required; others, like most Virginia delegates, sought a revision so thorough as to constitute a fresh start on different principles. Thus Randolph, using what Madison called "strong colours," referred bluntly to "the imbecility of the existing Confederacy." To cling to the "ordinary cautions," he said, would be "treason" to the Republic. Appropriate action must be taken or "the people will yield to despair" (Madison 1966, 16 June, 127–29).

Charles Pinckney of South Carolina, one of the younger delegates at Philadelphia—and in after years a frequent writer about its significance—also saw the confederation as totally inadequate. "Our Government," he said, "is despised, our laws robbed of their terrors. . . . Our foreign politics are as much deranged as our domestic economy. Our friends are slackened in their affections and our citizens loosened from their obedience" (Farrand 1966, 3:106–7, 427).

Oliver Ellsworth, a Connecticut delegate, reporting later to his state's ratifying convention, deplored how even "the morals of the people had been depraved for the want of an efficient government." Observing this lack, he cried out like an Old Testament prophet, "Iniquity has come in upon us like an overwhelming flood!" (Farrand 1966, 3:242). Noah Webster, who had studied law with Ellsworth in Hartford, called the Congress "a farce, a burlesque, a reproach" in lecture tours from Portsmouth to Charleston (Babbidge 1967, 6).

Hamilton, too, found the Articles of Confederation "feeble and precarious," the "petty states . . . jarring, jealous, and perverse," while Washington saw nothing but trouble ahead for "thirteen independent sovereignties eternally counteracting each other" (Canfield, 132).

It was not only American patriots who feared an abrupt and tragic end to their experiment. Apprehension and skepticism spread abroad. The French charge d'affaires, Louis Otto, who was paid to inform Versailles about conditions in America, reported that, in spite of the talents and patriotism of many delegates, especially Washington and Franklin, the convention was unlikely to succeed (Miller 1975, 212). Diverse commercial interests, varied customs, and jealousies would probably prevent unity.

Criticisms of the operations of the Articles of Confederation were especially vigorous during the first few weeks of the meeting. On 19 June, for example, Madison openly charged New Jersey with "a most notorious" violation of the Articles. The timing of his charge was probably not accidental; on that day the convention considered the alternative plan proposed by the New Jersey delegation. Madison proceeded, step by step, to assail the New Jersey plan, in general and in particular, under eight specific objections. He spoke at unusual length and appears to have aimed at a knock-out. He spoke of "unrighteous projects," of the "injustice" and "impotence" of state laws, of "pernicious machinations." The New Jersey plan, Madison concluded, was like a cobweb "which could entangle the weak but would be the sport of the strong." After Madison's speech, New Jersey kept the support only of New York and Delaware. The other states preferred the Virginia plan, by seven votes to three (Madison 1966, 19 June, 141).

THE LAST CHANCE

The leading delegates at Philadelphia believed they were engaged in a task of high statecraft. They regarded the difficult problem of devising a suitable republican form of government as important—not only for their own country but for all mankind. As Roger Sherman, the Connecticut cobbler, later told the first session of the first U.S. Congress, "This Government is different, and intended by the people to be different."

At the convention, concluding an involved, argumentative speech, Madison spoke of the last chance. "It is more than probable," he said solemnly, "that we are now digesting a plan which in its operation will decide forever the fate of a republican form of government." Hamilton agreed, using almost identical words. "If," he warned, "we do not give to that form due stability and wisdom, it will be disgraced among ourselves, disgraced and lost to mankind forever" (Madison 1966, 26 June, 195–96).

And the younger Pinckney, just before the Independence Day recess, sounded the same fearful yet hopeful warning: This convention, he warned, is "the last appeal." The dissolution of the Continental Congress, he said, had been prevented only by the prospect of the coming Philadelphia meeting (Madison, 2 July 232).

On July 18, the convention took up a Virginia resolution that provided that the United States guarantee each state a republican constitution and its existing laws. This seemingly simple and harmless pledge sparked an extended array of hopes and fears.

An unusually large number of delegates took part in the discussion. Gouverneur Morris of Pennsylvania found the proposal "very objectionable" and said that he was most unwilling to guarantee "such [bad] laws as exist in Rhode Island." However, Wilson, also of Pennsylvania, supported the resolution. Its purpose, he said, was "merely to secure the states against dangerous commo-

tions, insurrections, and rebellions." Mason of Virginia immediately came to Wilson's aid. If the national government, he said,
had no right to suppress rebellions it "must remain a passive
spectator of its own subversion."

Martin, the chief Maryland spokesman, formed an unusual
partnership with Morris. He was for allowing each state "to suppress its own rebellions."

Now Massachusetts joined the argument as Nathaniel Gorham
(no doubt recalling Shays' Rebellion) used words almost identical
to those of Mason. Gorham found it strange that a rebellion,
perhaps even an effort to "erect the standard of Monarchy," could
leave the national government "an inactive witness of its own
destruction."

At the end Wilson proposed a clarifying amendment, which was
forthwith adopted without objection as the day's session ended.
With only slight subsequent editing, that much-disputed section
now rests quietly in Article 4, Section 4, of the United States
Constitution (Madison 1966, 18 July, 320–21). The United States
guarantees to each state a republican form of government, protection against foreign invasion, and (on request by the state) protection against serious internal disturbances.

The fears of the framers continued to the very end of the
meeting. On the penultimate day of the convention, Colonel
George Mason reviewed the work of the convention at some
length and with extreme apprehension. In particular the proposed methods of amending the constitution evoked his anxieties.
Two methods of amending the document, he noticed, were provided. Either method required at some stage the assent of Congress. That meant, Mason declared, that no proper amendments
"would ever be obtained by the people" even if "the Government
became oppressive as he verily believed would be the case."

Just before the order to engross the completed text to make it
ready for signature, Mason announced that he would not sign it.
The proposed structures, he insisted, were "dangerous." These
dangers were, in Mason's view, two-fold: first to the liberties of the
people and second to the security of private property. This Virginia gentleman, with a growing estate of 76,000 acres, predicted
that the powers established by the constitution would end either
in a monarchy or in a tyrannical aristocracy (Collier and Collier
1986, 251). Mason was not sure, he admitted, which of these two
calamities would ensue, but he was certain it would be one or the
other (Madison 1966, 15 September, 651).

Few important predictions in American history have been so

wide off the mark. The amending process, the most important source of Mason's objections, has worked as planned; in fact, ten amendments to the Constitution (often known as the Bill of Rights) were adopted within two years. Two thousand amendments have been proposed, considered, and—in fourteen more cases—adopted at intervals during the Constitution's two centuries of service.

* * *

FRANKLIN: COURAGE AND CAUTION

The delegates feared what loomed ahead and were uncertain how to forestall the perils they feared. Their direct experience in the revolution and its aftermath left them with a queasy mixture of hope and fear. Franklin had a slightly different background.

Having lived and worked in France for nine of the past eleven years, Franklin had limited first-hand experience under the Articles of Confederation. Still, he had closely observed some of its operations, particularly in foreign affairs. He knew from observation, if not from direct personal experience, how it had faltered. He had, moreover, direct experience in the Congress of 1775–76, preceded by a long unhappy experience in dealing with a succession of Pennsylvania's colonial governors. Such experience had left him with one solid legacy: a resolute hostility to unlimited executive power. Franklin would be inclined to conclude with Montesquieu that "Every man who has power is impelled to abuse it," and so to agree with his colleague, James Madison, that "All men having power ought to be mistrusted" (quoted in Seldes, 753).

Franklin's political views centered on popular government, a broad suffrage, proportional representation, and rational cooperation. Sam Adams, off in Boston, insisted that Franklin was really "a Tory at heart." Like other straight-laced radicals, Adams thought that no man could be as much at home in Europe as Franklin was and yet remain pure in either his personal life or his revolutionary ardor. And Franklin did agree with Lord Kames, author of *Principles of Equity*, that the ownership of property derived from honest toil is a natural right (Miller 1975, 152–53).

In the convention Franklin could argue strongly against limiting the suffrage to property owners and yet be wary of absolute trust in "the collective wisdom." He endorsed neither Jefferson's explicit faith in a popular capacity for self-government, nor Hamilton's aristocratic creed, nor Adams' despair at the shortage of vigilance and virtue among ordinary people.

Franklin believed that public opinion, though impaired by interest, indolence, and ignorance, was yet the best path to public order and individual happiness. Experience abroad had led him to repudiate royal traditions of enormous emoluments for great offices. He resisted dictatorial powers, even in war-time, even for his much-admired commander-in-chief.

There is no persuasive evidence that Franklin cared much about the multitudinous operating details that the convention had to confront and settle. About two-thirds of all issues were so controversial as to require a recorded roll-call vote by the participating states. Franklin, meanwhile, seemed willing to acquiesce in, if not to support, almost any proposal that would produce an effective government (Collier and Collier 1986, 89).

One book on Franklin's political views contains a short chapter on "Dice, Chess, and Politics" (Connor 1965, 10–13). Franklin preferred chess. He had, in France, sat up all night over the sixty-four black and white squares, and one of his French *bagatelles* was entitled "Morals of Chess." The game, he wrote, developed "very valuable qualities of the mind." Dice, on the other hand, were "merely an idle amusement," deliberately designed to be utterly unpredictable. At chess, one may prevail by skill, reflection, and foresight; at dice no amount of thought will overcome the effects of blind chance.

Franklin clearly preferred to play his own personal game of life according to a set of rules, even if those regulations were arbitrary. During the State debates on ratification, Franklin wrote to a friend in France that a plan of government was not shaped "as a game of chess may be played, by a skillful hand, without a fault." Because conflicting opinions and interests give rise to misunderstandings, "the wisest must agree to some unreasonable things so that reasonableness of more consequence may be obtained." Altogether, Franklin concluded after experiencing his final and greatest consultation, the drafting of the Constitution was like a game of backgammon in which both choice and chance had a part (Wood 1969, 593; Van Doren 1938, 771–72).

In his crafty and brief address for the closing day of the convention, the final and in some respects the most memorable public statement of his career, Franklin included these words, "There is no form of government but what may be a blessing to the people *if well administered.*"

Franklin had some basic ideas of his own to contribute to the convention debates. In addition, he played the role of the honest broker, driving toward compromise and conciliation among a group of younger, more militant partisans. It was an essential role that none could play better than he.

The early eighteenth-century English poet, Alexander Pope, was part of Franklin's enormous reading list. Pope is praised as "one of our best Writers" in Franklin's recommended curriculum for the College of Pennsylvania. A couplet in Pope's *Essay On Man* (Epistle 3, line 303) summarized Franklin's political views:

> For forms of Government, let Fools contest
> Whate'er is best administered is best.

Franklin's appeal in his closing speech at the convention provided a curious echo of the poet, as he urged his colleagues to sign the Constitution and "turn our future thoughts and endeavors to the means of having it *well-administered*" (appendix A5).

8
Chronology: Prologue and Organization

Note: This chapter and the four that follow it divide the chronology of the convention into five episodes, as follows:

Chapter 8, "Prologue and Organization," the first episode through 28 May 1787, includes relevant events just before the convention, the drafting and adoption of its rules, and the election of its officers.

Chapter 9, "Rival Plans," relates the presentation of the Virginia Plan, including the vexed issue of representation in the legislature (29 May), followed by discussion of its provisions. New Jersey offered (15–16 June) a rival and different plan.

Chapter 10, "Compromise on Representation," describes the failure of either plan to gain united support and the decision of the convention (2 July) to elect as a last resort a committee with one member from each state to develop a compromise. The debate on the compromise proposals ended with their approval (16 July) by the narrowest possible margin.

Chapter 11, "Other Issues," recounts how the Convention turned to other topics, impeachment procedures (20 July), presidential tenure (26 July), voting qualifications (7 August), and regulation of the slave trade (25 August), among others. A small Committee on Style was then named; it reported 12 September.

Chapter 12, "Decisions and Epilogue," describes how the convention, now moving toward adjournment, considered many last-minute suggestions, rejecting most of them. It approved a letter of transmittal, ceremonially signed the engrossed Constitution, and sent it off to Congress to initiate the process of ratification (13–18 September, 12–13 December 1787, and 4 July 1788).

These chapters do not list all the deliberations, debates, and decisions of the Constitutional Convention. They concentrate, in the main, on a day-by-day account of the involvement of Benjamin Franklin. However, a very few general convention transactions, even if not directly related to Franklin's activities, have been included for convenient reference.

1785

14 SEPTEMBER   Franklin arrived Philadelphia from Paris, Le Havre, and Southampton, completing his eighth Atlantic crossing.

11 OCTOBER   Nominated by all major groups, Franklin was elected to the Pennsylvania Supreme Executive Council.

29 OCTOBER   Franklin elected President, Pennsylvania Supreme Executive Council. He was reelected in 1786 and 1787.

1786

7 AUGUST   Continental Congress discussed revision of the Articles of Confederation.

14 SEPTEMBER   Five states meeting in Annapolis recommend a convention to meet in May 1787. Although he did not attend the Annapolis meeting, Franklin was fully aware that the Articles of Confederation were not satisfactory and equally sure that their defects would be remedied.

24 NOVEMBER   In a letter Franklin prophetically assured an English friend, "Errors in our Constitutions . . . we shall mend."

30 DECEMBER   Seven Pennsylvania deputies chosen by the assembly to attend the Constitutional Convention.

1787

17 JANUARY   Franklin's eighty-first birthday. "All would live long; none would grow old," as Poor Richard said some thirty years earlier. To his contemporaries, the longevity of the oldest delegate to the Constitutional Convention probably seemed even more remarkable than it does today. The average life expectancy for Massachusetts-born males was under forty years in 1707. The comparable figure would rise to forty-seven years in 1900, to sixty-eight years in 1950, in 1983 to seventy-four years (Schick 1986, 1).

The average signer of the Constitution, having survived the perils of colonial infancy, lived to age sixty-seven; Franklin died at eighty-four. His long lifespan had solid hereditary precedents; his father lived until eighty-five, his mother to eighty-nine, his maternal grandfather to eighty-three, his paternal grandfather in England to eighty-four, and his patronymic Uncle Ben to seventy-seven.

4 FEBRUARY   Massachusetts state forces crushed and dispersed Shays' Rebellion.

21 FEBRUARY   Congress voted to summon the Convention, to meet on May 14 at Philadelphia.

17 MARCH   Franklin signed a Proclamation offering, on behalf of the Commonwealth of Pennsylvania, a reward for the apprehension of Daniel Shays and of certain rebels associated with him (Ferris and Charleton 1986, 20).

Shays, an Army captain during the revolution, had organized and led as many as two thousand men who attacked the federal arsenal at Springfield, Massachusetts, and forced some state courts to disband. The rebels, mostly farmers, having met severe difficulties from increased farm taxes and post-war economic dislocations, faced foreclosures, loss of homes and subsistence, and debtor's prison. The state requested national help but the response of the Continental Congress was, as usual, little and lethargic.

The rebellion stirred fears of civil disorders throughout the country. Although it was soon ended by state forces, it revealed the extent of suffering and disaffection among ordinary people. Shays' Rebellion became a well-publicized symbol of the need to strengthen the national government.

28 MARCH   By supplemental act, the General Assembly added Franklin to the Pennsylvania delegation (Farrand 1966, 3:567).

Parton (1971, 2:565) explained that this addition made available "one man whom all could concur in calling to the Chair" in case Washington decided not to attend. Although Franklin ultimately attended regularly, he "at first doubted that his health would permit him to serve" (Van Doren 1943, 4). He had recently helped to form the new Society for Political Enquiries, which included several other convention delegates.

9 APRIL   Washington accepted appointment as a Virginia delegate, protesting, however, that "my consent goes contrary to my judgment" (Emery 1976, 302).

13 MAY (SUNDAY)   Washington arrived at Philadelphia. His first call was to the new home of Benjamin Franklin. This would be the fifth, and most extended meeting of the two men. As their first postwar meeting, it probably involved a certain amount of protocol conversation. Washington was visiting Pennsylvania. In a

sense the President of the Pennsylvania Council was the official host for the coming Constitutional Convention. Thus, Washington's visit to Franklin "as soon as I got to town" (as he wrote in his diary) was an appropriate courtesy.

The two met in Franklin's garden, under the mulberry tree. The area around Franklin's garden was cluttered by building material and debris; Franklin was having some nearby houses rebuilt.

The last time these two men had met was in October 1775, when Franklin led a Committee of the Continental Congress to Cambridge, Massachusetts, to confer with Washington and the New England authorities about the support of the Continental Army. In the twelve-year interval, the Declaration of Independence had been issued, the Revolutionary War fought and won, and the Treaty of Paris negotiated. Surely these two old comrades, whose acquaintance had begun thirty-two years earlier when they aided Braddock's ill-fated expedition against Fort Duquesne and planned a road between Philadelphia and Winchester (Van Doren 1938, 261), found many other things to discuss that sunny Sunday afternoon besides protocol.

14 MAY (MONDAY) In keeping with the Congress's track record, the date set for the convention arrived with only two of thirteen states represented. Lacking a quorum for the scheduled convention, the Virginia delegation met every morning. In the afternoons they joined the Pennsylvania delegation for informal talks. This may have been the first occasion on which Franklin and Madison met, although Madison, who had been in town since 3 May, could have already called on Franklin (Burns 1982, 33; I. Brant 1950, 17; Farrand 1966, 3:500).

That day, again according to his diary, Washington dined with Franklin (Van Doren 1938, 744).

Informal talks continued all week, into the following Monday, and perhaps longer (Farrand 1966, 3:21).

15 MAY (TUESDAY) The state seal was affixed to the document naming the Pennsylvania delegation (Farrand 1966, 3:567).

16 MAY (WEDNESDAY) Franklin gave a dinner for delegates who had arrived in Philadelphia. The convention was, however, still short of its quorum, so the guests probably did not fully occupy the twenty-four-seat capacity of Franklin's new dining room (Aldridge 1767, 391). Few or many, the guests opened and noisily enjoyed a cask of porter provided by Franklin's friend, Thomas

Jordan (Farrand 1966, 3:20). Washington's diary records that the general drank tea that evening but that need not exclude the possibility that he drank some porter, too.

Gossips meanly said that "Poor Richard" gave the welcome dinner early, to minimize the expense before more delegates arrived (Fay 1929, 504).

25 MAY (FRIDAY)   A quorum having at last assembled, the Constitutional Convention organized itself by electing a president and a secretary, employing a messenger and a doorkeeper (Farrand 1913, 57), registering the credentials, and electing a committee to draft rules of procedure.

Franklin missed the formal opening session. There were light rains and gusty winds. Madison (1966, 24) wrote that "the state of the weather and of his health confined him to his house." Franklin had made alternative arrangements with Robert Morris so that his wish to see Washington in the President's chair was fulfilled (Clark 1983, 408). According to Madison, the nomination of Washington "came with peculiar grace from Pennsylvania as Doc'r Franklin alone could have been thought of as a competitor."

Washington had accepted appointment as a Virginia delegate late, and with considerable reluctance. He feared the convention might fail and, in doing so, cloud his shining national reputation. His exchanges of anxious letters with such friends as John Jay in New York and Henry Knox in Massachusetts led him to advise the latter, "In confidence I inform you it is not at this time my purpose to attend" (Emery 1976, 300). However, unlike his old friend, Patrick Henry, Washington did not completely and finally refuse.

When, after weeks of doubtful delay, he finally accepted Virginia Governor Randolph's appointment, his letter was so filled with *if*s, and *might*s, and *provided*s that the governor would read it with care to make sure that Washington's answer was affirmative. Besides, Washington wrote, he was suffering from rheumatism. The pain in his shoulder, if it worsened, might prevent his travel. Indeed, his attendance at Philadelphia has been described by a recent writer as the "major gamble of his life; no one had more to lose than he" (Wills 1984, 156).

As convention president, however, Washington could avoid public involvement in the expected strife of the convention, keep silent on the issues, at least until a successful outcome was assured, and rely on the austere impartiality required of the presidency to isolate him from any undesirable outcomes. Perhaps—and this last is surmise—the presidency of the convention was among the topics discussed by Washington and Franklin during their conversations in Franklin's garden and dining room.

To the post of convention secretary, Major William Jackson was elected over Pennsylvania's nominee, Temple Franklin, Benjamin Franklin's grandson. The vote was 7-2.

The election of Major Jackson over Temple Franklin could hardly have been a surprise. Jackson had made a career in the military and diplomatic services. After the Battle of Charleston, Jackson became a diplomatic aide to Henry Laurens, assigned briefly to Amsterdam. Since Holland was at war with England in 1780, a Dutch loan to America, with French security, was negotiated. Jackson clashed with Franklin about the handling of the Dutch funds. Jackson later had the wisdom and grace to withdraw his criticisms, with apologies to Franklin (Van Doren 1938, 623, 626, 744). After the war Jackson became an active leader in the Cincinnati and maintained his reputation for punctillious military etiquette.

In April 1787 Jackson sought the Philadelphia appointment in a letter to Washington at Mount Vernon (Farrand 1966, 3:18; Aldridge 1965, 316). In May, when Washington reached Chester, Jackson was one of a small contingent of officers waiting to escort the general, in style, on the last leg of his journey to the convention city.

George Mason was one of several delegates who knew about Jackson's wish for the appointment. He felt that there would be little compensation except the introduction "to something more substantial" (Farrand 1966, 3:24). Mason's position on the appointment is not known but he and Franklin were important opponents in the protracted Virginia-Pennsylvania rivalry over the control of the Ohio country (Miller 1975, 181).

Temple Franklin was nominated by a delegate from Pennsylvania. Jackson was nominated by Alexander Hamilton speaking for the New York delegation. New York delegate, Lansing, who also kept a partial log of the convention, reported that Jackson, after lobbying urgently for the appointment, was waiting expectantly outside the meeting hall. Immediately after the election Jackson was "called in" and took an assigned seat (Strayer 1939, 22).

In view of such circumstances it is just possible—but it must be no more than a conjecture—to suppose that Franklin's absence from the formal opening session to elect Washington and Jackson as convention officers was not solely due to either "heavy rain" or to temporary illness.

Most students of the Convention, contemporary and later, agree that Jackson did not produce a very helpful account of its transactions. Had it not been for Madison's voluntary and unpaid services in taking notes, we would be very poorly informed of what happened.

John Quincy Adams in 1818, as Monroe's secretary of state, tried with little success to secure from Jackson a better understanding of the documentation of the official convention records. Jackson told Adams that, in disposing of convention records, he was carrying out the wishes of George Washington. This policy, "he supposed, had been a loss to him of many thousand dollars" (Farrand 1966, 3:426).

Jared Sparks, the president of Harvard in 1831, evaluated Jackson's services in an outspoken letter to Madison. "Your Secretary of the Convention," he concluded, "was a very stupid Secretary not to take care of those things [the Convention papers] better and to make a better journal than the dry bones which now go by that name" (Farrand 1966 3:514). A modern historian has made an equally devastating appraisal of Jackson's work. He "turned out to be lazy and inefficient and his Journal is unreliable" (Bernstein 1987, 152).

It is tempting to speculate how understanding of the convention and of the Constitution might be improved by a record better than that produced by Jackson's formal and minimal notes. The younger Franklin, it seems safe to say, would have worked under the close and encouraging scrutiny of his grandfather. And he would have brought to the Philadelphia convention the valuable experience gained by serving as the secretary of the American delegation at meetings in Paris.

We do not know for sure which two delegations cast their votes for Temple Franklin. The vote by the states on the election is one of the very few roll calls that Madison's *Notes* do not record. Presumably Pennsylvania was one of them. A document called the "secret Proceedings" by New York delegate Yates states that Pennsylvania was the only state supporting Temple Franklin for convention secretary (Farrand 1966, 3:410).

In spite of the great prestige of his grandfather, Temple Franklin was not an invincible candidate. In Paris he had not always been attentive to his duties. Worse, Benjamin Franklin's critics circulated doubts in Congress regarding the young man's loyalty. The grandfather reacted promptly and indignantly to these innuendos. He cautiously predicted that his grandson *"may in time* become of great service to his country" (emphasis added). Then, in evident pain and anger, the old man added, "It is enough that I have lost my son. Would they add my grandson?" But in an election, any accusation, even if malicious, may have an adverse effect (Fleming 1972, 306, 3813–4).

In addition to the impact of his own smudged record, young Franklin's selection would not have been helped by the fact that his father, William Franklin, had been a royal governor of New Jersey, a devoted loyalist throughout the revolution, regarded as "a virulent enemy," a condemned and imprisoned Tory traitor to the rebel cause, and was now living in England on a pension.

That evening Gouverneur Morris told a friend, who told another friend, that Jackson was "extremely delighted and thinks his fortune and fame are both established" by the election. Morris also reported "Old Dr. F. much mortified that he had not enough [influence] to procure the place for his Grandson." The conclusion about Jackson's glee seems reasonable but the account of Franklin's chagrin is less easy to accept. Since Franklin was not at the convention that day, Morris apparently described his feelings from supposition or hearsay. In either case, the comment shows that, on this issue at least, the Pennsylvania delegation was not unamimous (Historians 1987, 10). Besides, Major Jackson resided close at hand in Philadelphia, whereas Temple Franklin was miles away up the Delaware on a New Jersey farm.

26 MAY (SATURDAY)   Although the meeting is not explicitly reported, the convention Rules Committee must have met this day to prepare its report.

28 MAY (MONDAY)   Franklin and some other delegates took their seats in convention for the first time.

The Rules Committee proposed, and the convention adopted, some rules of procedure, including a rule of secrecy regarding the subjects discussed and opinions expressed. With minor exceptions, this rule was strictly observed. The secrecy rule was approved without objection. Sentries were posted at the doorways (Farrand 1966, 1:6).

The Rules did not forbid the secretary or any other participant from keeping a record of what was said and done. They did ban the printing, publication, or communication of what was spoken in convention.

However, (Bowen 1974, 22) "it seemed impossible to keep old Dr. Franklin quiet." It has been said that some discreet member of the convention was assigned to attend Franklin's convivial dinners, heading the conversation in a safer direction if the senior delegate, during one of his anecdotes, approached the revelation of some secret. Van Doren (1943, 159) however, calls this account a "grotesque legend." It is unlikely that any delegate would presume to serve as censor of the eminent Dr. Franklin; it is even more implausible that the president of the state Supreme Council would tolerate such tutelage.

Jefferson, kept away by his duties as our ambassador in Paris, heard about the list of delegates and declared the Convention "an assembly of demi-gods." However Jefferson's demi-gods made, he thought, a major error in adopting the secrecy rule. It was, he said, "an abominable precedent." The demi-gods on the ground were also on the spot; they had no misgivings about secrecy. The Freedom of Information Act was nearly two hundred years in the future. Secrecy, in 1787, among its other advantages, made it easier for delegates to change their minds and thus to reach agreements.

The secrecy rule was accepted and obeyed by all the delegates, including George Mason who is generally regarded as the convention's chief spokesman for including a Bill of Rights in the Constitution.

That evening Franklin received the twenty-eight-year-old Noah Webster, already widely known for his hopeful career as the nation's first and most famous lexicographer. He and Franklin had met a year before and corresponded about spelling reform that Franklin had proposed nearly twenty years earlier. Webster had served briefly in the revolution, had published his famous "blue-back" speller, and now showed a lively and genuine interest in public affairs.

This was the first of several visits to Franklin's house by Noah Webster during the convention. On this occasion Webster was accompanied by "some ladies"—almost certainly Mrs. Duncan Ingraham of Philadelphia and her house guest and younger sister, Rebecca Greenleaf of Boston, whom Webster was assiduously courting. He would marry Rebecca in two years (Historians 1987, 13; Warfel 1936, 163).

Meanwhile, at the convention, a quorum of delegates had presented their credentials, their elected officers were in place, their rules had been adopted, and a great debate would begin the next morning.

9
Chronology: Rival Plans

1787

29 MAY (TUESDAY) The substantive work of the Convention began when Governor Randolph presented the "Virginia Plan."

30 MAY (WEDNESDAY) The convention met as a Committee of the Whole, with Gorham of Massachusetts in the chair. This respected Boston merchant had just arrived from congressional service in New York City, having observed his forty-ninth birthday on Sunday.

During his chairmanship, the convention for the next two weeks discussed the Virginia Plan in the form of a series of resolutions. Franklin was soon identified, along with Madison, Wilson, and others, as favoring a national government. Franklin was optimistic at this stage, calling the convention "the most august and respectable assembly" (Brant 1950, 31).

31 MAY (THURSDAY) Franklin made his first statement from the floor suggesting that the states should not have power to enact laws contrary to the provisions of international treaties (Van Doren 1938, 745). This motion by the nation's most experienced diplomat, "whose eyes always looked beyond American shores" (McLaughlin, 57) was at once unanimously approved. (The Constitution, Article 6, says "this Constitution . . . and all Treaties made, or which shall be made, under the Authority of the United States, shall be the Supreme Law of the Land.")

Franklin next joined the Pennsylvania delegation in voting nay on a resolution by Madison: "that the national legislature ought to consist of two branches."

Madison correctly thought the Pennsylvania dissent was meant mainly to please Franklin. Although most of the Pennsylvania delegation preferred a two-house legislature, Franklin's belief in a unicameral legislature was not a slight or transient preference. He told the Pennsylvania Constitutional Convention in 1776 that having a legislature with two Chambers was like hitching horses at both ends of a wagon. If the horses were indolent and feeble the cart would simply stand still; if they were strong and energetic they would tear the cart to pieces (Aldridge 1965, 261).

1 JUNE, (FRIDAY)   A Virginia Resolution was considered providing for a national executive elected by Congress. It was moved and seconded that the executive be one person. After "a considerable pause," Franklin urged delegates to speak up before the motion was put. Van Doren offers a reasonable explanation for the silence among delegates who, on all other topics, exhibited little reticence. "The gentlemen had been slow to speak because it was hard . . . to think of a single executive without thinking of a king" (Van Doren 1943, 53).

Nevertheless Delegates Rutledge, Sherman, Wilson, Gerry, Randolph, Wilson (again), and Madison all responded to Franklin's suggestion.

2 JUNE (SATURDAY)   Franklin moved that the executive should have necessary expenses defrayed but receive "no salary, stipend, fee, or reward" (appendix A1).

Honors and profits, he said, are the respective goals of ambition and avarice. To combine the two dangers in "profitable pre-eminence" threatens disaster. In one of the many biblical allusions with which Franklin often pointed a moral, he said that rulers would, if they could, follow the example of Pharoah—take all the people's money and all their lands, and at last enslave them and their children.

He continued with four examples—two from the United States and two from abroad—of successful public service without financial rewards.

1. In England, a high sheriff is an honorable, but not a profitable, post. Yet it is well-executed "usually by some of the principal Gentlemen of the County."

2. In France it is an honor to be a counsellor. The cost of obtaining the post exceeds the income from the fees collected. Respect is motive enough to render public service "without the mean inducement of pecuniary satisfaction."

3. The Quakers use committees from their periodic sessions to resolve disputes without law suits. Their service is not rewarded by salaries and perquisities—"the less the profit, the greater the honor."

4. General Washington served for eight years of wartime fa-

tigues, anxieties, and distresses with no salary. Are we unable to find three or four men who would serve an equal term in peace to see that our laws are faithfully executed? "Sir, I have a better opinion of our Country."

Franklin probably did not expect his amendment to be adopted, for he closed with these words, "If it [his proposal] is not seconded or accepted I must be contented with the satisfaction of having delivered my opinion frankly and done my duty."

Franklin's proposal was, however, seconded by Hamilton, merely, he said, to bring "so respectable a proposition before the Committee" (Van Doren 1938, 745). There was no further discussion and no action. Madison noted that it "was treated with great respect" because of its author, but the convention did not regard it as either timely or practical.

Delegates who knew Franklin's political views would not regard his amendment as a hare-brained scheme by a senile revolutionary (Historians 1987, 21). They would see it as matured judgment based on long experience with the British Parliament. In 1784, for example, Franklin wrote to an English friend:

"In my humble Opinion, the Root of the Evil [in Britain] lies in the enormous Salaries, Emoluments and Patronage of your great Offices and . . . you will never be at rest until they are all abolish'd and every place of Honour made at the same time, instead of a place of Profit, a place of Expence and burthen" (Fleming 1972, 364).

Franklin probably knew, since it was a matter of public record, that Washington had recently declined with thanks a grateful gift for his services to his country. The Virginia Legislature had voted to convey to Washington shares in Navigation Companies on the James and the Potomac. Washington wrote to Governor Patrick Henry, "I thought it my duty to join a firm resolution to shut my hand against every pecuniary recompense. To this resolution (if I had the inclination) I do not consider myself at liberty to depart" (Powers 1976, 111).

4 JUNE (MONDAY)   Virginia Resolution 8 called for a Council of Revision, composed of "the national executive and a convenient number of the national judiciary" with authority to review all the acts of the national legislature.

Franklin opposed an executive veto, citing the Pennsylvania colonial experience (appendix B1).

Wilson mentioned in passing Franklin's proposal about the president's compensation.

Mason said that Franklin's position on the veto was "based on experience, the best of all tests."

Rufus King quoted Franklin as declaring, "We ought not to believe that one man can possess more wisdom than both branches of the Legislature" (Farrand 1966, 1:107).

Franklin then cited the Dutch experience with excessive executive power (appendix B2).

He and Roger Sherman were the only two 1787 delegates present who had worked with Jefferson in 1776 to revise the draft of the Declaration of Independence. They could have reminded one another that the very first item in their indictment against George III for his "repeated injuries and usurpations" was: "He has refused his Assent to Laws, the most wholesome and necessary for the public good."

The Virginia resolution was unanimously rejected. So was a slightly milder substitute by Butler, although seconded by Franklin, that the executive have power to suspend the application of any legislative act "for a period of years."

(In the end in Article 1, Section 7, Clause 2, the Constitution provided for an executive veto that may be bypassed by a two-thirds vote in each House.)

5 JUNE (TUESDAY)   The convention discussed the judicial branch of the new government. Franklin urged that no decision be made until all possible methods of choosing federal judges had been examined. In Scotland, Franklin said with mock gravity (appendix B3), the sixteen Lords of Session who comprise the highest court were nominated by the barristers. These lawyers always placed the most able members of their profession on the bench; thus they might gain a share in their rivals' extensive legal practice.

Franklin's "Scottish mode" was, of course, a hoax—part of his extensive life-long collection. It would be immediately recognized as such by all present except, perhaps, Major Jackson. The interpellation no doubt caused a relaxing laugh among the delegates, nearly all of whom had legal training.

Wilson of Pennsylvania and Rutledge of South Carolina had clashed head-on that morning about the method of appointing judges. Franklin's light intervention may have provided the occasion for Madison's immediate motion, seconded by Wilson, to postpone the controversial issue.

6 JUNE (WEDNESDAY)   Franklin had George Washington and Dr. William Samuel Johnson, a newly-arrived Connecticut delegate, among his guests at dinner (Van Doren 1938, 190, 741; Walsh

1935, 186, 205). Johnson, a former loyalist, but now thoroughly rehabilitated, would become chairman of the convention Committee on Style.

8 JUNE (SATURDAY) Franklin sent Granville Sharp, the British abolitionist who had brought the Somersett case into English courts (see chapter 6, note 2), a copy of the bylaws of the Pennsylvania Anti-Slavery Society (Historians 1987, 30). Franklin had just become its President (Van Doren 1938, 741).

11 JUNE (MONDAY) Franklin urged delegates to avoid rancor in the debate on relations between the small states and the larger ones (appendix A2).

Franklin went on to minimize the importance of the issue. Small states, he said, have many advantages. He would not greatly object to giving parts of Pennsylvania to New Jersey and Delaware, thus diminishing the differences of area and population. Coming from the president of Pennsylvania, this must have been a startling declaration, showing how firmly he believed in the need for union.

He even submitted a formula of his own: (1) The weakest state declares what portion of its resources it can and will furnish for the Union; (2) the other states agree to supply an equal proportion; (3) funds thus accumulated are at the disposition of Congress; (4) Congress, with an equal number of delegates from each state, allots the funds by majority vote of individual members; (5) if the combined funds are not enough, Congress may request further voluntary funds from the richer and more powerful states.

This rather complex scheme, still lacking much essential detail, Franklin called an "accommodating proposition." It has been described by one historian (Warren 1967, 209) as "so impractical in form as to warrant the suspicion that it was put forward simply to distract the minds of the delegates."

Whether the proposal was fundamental or merely diversionary, there can be little doubt of the impact of Franklin's closing remarks. To those who still insisted that the one-state-one-vote formula was consecrated and unchangeable, Franklin simply quoted one sentence adopted by the Continental Congress of 1774. It showed that the formula had been accepted by the Congress because that body did not then have at hand a means to assess the relative importance of each colony.

Franklin was in England in 1774 but he still recalled in 1787 the terms of the earliest decision on representation and could quote it with effect (appendix A2).

This was the first day of a spell of hot weather. It happened also to be the day when the delegates who lodged at the Indian Queen tavern gave a dinner for their colleagues. Franklin was invited in his role as president of Pennsylvania. As far as we know, he attended. His written invitation was wrongly dated "Wednesday, June 7." In the year 1787, June 7 fell on a Thursday. The dinner was announced for "next Monday" without a date. The date on the invitation is probably some harried copyist's error.

12 JUNE (TUESDAY)   The question of pay for members of Congress was raised. The motion provided for "liberal and fixed compensation for members" of the House of Representatives. Franklin (appendix B4) said he favored "fixed" but not "liberal." The offending word was deleted without dissent, leaving congressional salaries fixed but not (at least not yet) liberal.

Fay (1929, 504) says that "in spite of his [Franklin's] speech liberal salaries were attached to all Federal appointments." The Constitution, however, does not contain such language; it provides only that the president and the members of Congress and of the judiciary shall receive "a compensation" (Article 1, Section 6; Article 2, Section 1; Article 3, Section 1).

It appears that the convention, unable to agree that congressmen should be paid four dollars a day, avoided the issue by empowering Congress to determine its own salaries.

Gorham, in the debate, remarked sardonically that the state legislatures usually kept their salaries low to exclude more capable people from the contest. He said he felt sure, therefore, that Congress itself would not abuse the power to fix its members' compensation. Madison, however, insisted to the last that it was "indecent" for elected officials "to put their hands into the public purse for the sake of their own pockets" (Madison 1966, 178).

In the light of current legislation and developments in the pay, perquisites, and pensions of members of Congress and their heirs, dependents, and kinsfolk, it is hard not to feel sympathy for Franklin's repeated warnings about the escalation of the rewards of officials, especially those who determine their own compensation by the statutes and budgets they enact.

13 JUNE (WEDNESDAY)   The Committee of the Whole reported to the convention the Virginia Plan with numerous amendments (Farrand 1921, 82).

14 JUNE (THURSDAY)   A one-day adjournment was adopted to give time to develop a rival "federal" plan (Farrand 1921, 84). There was, however, no respite for busy Ben Franklin. He presided as usual over a meeting of the state Executive Council and

afterwards spent time again with the tireless Noah Webster, who brought with him James Greenleaf, Rebecca's brother, to call on his excellency, the president of Pennsylvania.

15 JUNE (FRIDAY)   The New Jersey Plan was offered as a substitute for the Virginia Plan. Both plans were referred to the Committee of the Whole (Farrand 1921, 85–86).

19 JUNE (TUESDAY)   A choice between the New Jersey "Federal" plan and the Virginia "National" plan was presented to the committee. The majority favored the Virginia plan by seven to three, with the vote of Maryland divided and so not counted (Farrand 1921, 89).

This preliminary vote, however, would not settle the issue of state representation in Congress. The convention, not a committee, must now debate this and other questions. The process would alternate walk-out threats and pleas for moderation, with incidential attention to other issues.

10

Chronology: Compromise on Representation

1787

26 JUNE (TUESDAY)   Franklin seconded General Pinckney's motion to pay no stipends to senators. Franklin pointed out that some younger members of the convention would probably be elected to the senate; people should not be able to charge that the delegates had "carved out" lucrative places for themselves (appendix B4).

The Pinckney-Franklin motion was narrowly defeated, 6-5. Pennsylvania voted for the motion. As Franklin predicted, about half of the delegates later became senators and congressmen.

When Franklin died three years later, the Senate, although urged to do so by both Jefferson and Madison, refused to join the House of Representatives in honoring his memory by wearing mourning for a month. In contrast, when the news reached Paris, the National Assembly voted unanimously to adopt ceremonial mourning[1] for "the philosopher who has most contributed to extend the rights of man over the whole earth" (Van Doren 1938, 780–81). But, of course, Franklin had never advised *French* legislators to refrain from carving out lucrative places.

27 JUNE (WEDNESDAY)   John Rutledge of South Carolina moved that the convention forthwith consider and act upon "the rules of suffrage in the two branches [of the Congress]." His motion was carried unanimously; both sides were ready to vote (Farrand 1921, 93).

28 JUNE (THURSDAY)   Late in the day Franklin offered his famous remarks suggesting that more progress would be made if each morning's session were opened by "imploring the assistance of heaven" (appendix A3). This was one of several convention speeches that Franklin seems to have delivered in person, speaking in a low voice, addressing his remarks to Washington almost as

though the two men were engaged in a personal conversation (Brant 1950, 84). Roger Sherman of Connecticut seconded the motion.

Delegate Williamson of North Carolina objected that the Constitutional Convention had no money to employ a chaplain.[2] The general opinion seemed to be, Franklin thought, that prayers were unnecessary (Bowen 1966, 7, 12).

Perhaps calling in a clergyman from the city at this stage, more than a month after the convention had begun, might have led the uninformed public to suspect the truth—that the convention was near a complete breakdown. Madison thought that there might have been some unspoken objection to the numerical strength of the Quakers in Philadelphia, as well as the possibility of some controversy in designating a chaplain since the convention included members of several denominations.

Hamilton, according to Madison's *Notes,* said that it was too late to initiate the practise of daily prayers. Franklin, Sherman, and others replied that past omission of a duty could not justify a further omission. Randolph then proposed that a sermon be preached the following week, on Independence Day, and daily prayers by offered thereafter. Franklin immediately seconded that motion.

Whether Franklin spoke from a genuine faith in the efficacy of prayer or merely to shift attention from quarrelsome issues to more solemn reflections, his suggestion at the very least surely and forcefully reminded all delegates of the basic importance of their work.

Bancroft, writing more than a century ago, concluded that Franklin's reference to "His concurring aid" implied "a purification from the domain of selfish interest." Bancroft also believed that the record of the next session shows that the delegates were in fact "less absorbed by inferior motives" (Bancroft 1884, 2:59).

In any case Washington, according to Madison's *Notes,* did not call, that day or later, for a vote on either Franklin's suggestion for daily prayer or on Randolph's alternative. It is not clear how motions duly made and seconded could be disregarded without a vote or some other recorded transaction.

As a group the delegates seem to have been entirely willing to avoid divisive new issues of church-state relations. No body of opinion had then been formed on whether complete religious freedom could be provided by popular government. The convention was able to agree no further than to forbid religious tests as a qualification for public offices. A desire to sidetrack the entire problem by avoiding debate on a symbolic ritual seems quite credible.

Fay satirizes Franklin's suggestion about prayer as "brief but moving, and filled with Biblical piety; [it] would have made the ladies at Passy weep, but it had no effect whatsoever on the American delegates" (1929, 504). He adds that the failure of the convention to act on the prayer proposal "was a lesson" for Franklin and that Franklin thereafter "was no longer deeply interested in the Convention" (1929, 505). Subsequent events scarcely justify this conclusion.

One or more delegates if so inclined, might have offered a daily prayer. Possibly some did so privately. Public prayer would not have infringed the convention's procedural rules. However no delegate attempted to appeal directly to Heaven in public without a clerical proxy.

Ten months later, in April 1788 during the state ratification debates, Franklin, in a letter to the *Federal Gazette* ((Farrand 1966, 3:296–97), referred again to providential influence on the convention. Franklin's purpose in sending this communication to the *Gazette* is not entirely clear. He did not mention his prayer motion of 28 June and he carefully disavowed any intention of claiming that the convention was divinely inspired. Yet, he continued, it was difficult to conceive that a task of such momentous importance to the population and posterity of a great nation could be conducted unless "in some degree influenced, guided, and governed by that omnipotent, omnipresent, and beneficent Ruler, in whom all inferior Spirits live and move and have their Being."

There exists another account of the prayer motion (Farrand 1966, 3:467–73). This account is in a letter written by William Steele to his son, Jonathan. The writer of this letter attributes his narrative "as nearly as I can recollect" to conversations with Jonathan Dayton, a New Jersey delegate, the youngest signer of the Constitution, speaker of the House of Representatives (1791–99) and U.S. senator (1799–1805). Dayton, after whom the Ohio city is named, was one of the early surveyors in that part of Ohio.

According to Dayton's account as related by Steele, Franklin's remarks recommending daily prayer came at the conclusion of his plea for compromise on the vexed issue of state representation in the Senate. Expressing surprise that the proposal had not been made earlier in the convention, Franklin suggested the appointment of a chaplain to open each day's session with a prayer that the Creator would "enlighten our minds with a portion of Heavenly wisdom, influence our hearts . . . and crown our labors with complete and abundant success." The president, and the other delegates, with one exception, showed in their countenances marked approbation of Franklin's proposals. The one exception according to Steele and Dayton, was "Mr. H___, from ___." (The only delegates whose last names began with the letter "H" were Alexander Hamilton of New York, William Churchill Houston of New Jersey, and William Houstoun of Georgia.) All three were present on 28 June. Houston did not speak at all on the convention record, attended only a few days, did not stay to sign the Constitution, and died within a year. Houstoun attended about forty days but spoke only half-a-dozen times. No doubt Steele intended to identify Hamilton. In a comment attributed to him by Steele, Hamilton is supposed to have impiously insisted that the delegates were "competent to transact the business . . . and . . . he did not see the necessity of calling in *foreign aid*."

The motion to approve a chaplain was then "instantly seconded and carried, whether under the silent disapprobation of Mr. H___, or his solitary negative, I do not recollect." Dayton did remember, still according to Steele, that the newly elected chaplain opened the next session with prayer, whereupon the deadlock on the disputed issue was averted and a compromise established.

William Steele closed his long letter by ascribing his information to personal conversations ten years earlier. "I may have differed much from General Dayton in his phraseology but am confident I have faithfully stated the *facts*," wrote Steele. He had hoped, he said, to persuade Dayton to make a written record of these significant events but "the hand of death has removed him."

Dayton died at Elizabeth, New Jersey, in 1824. Steele dated his letter to his son in 1825. The letter was published in the *National Intelligencer* in 1826. Hamilton had been killed in a duel with Aaron Burr in 1804.

In 1831 Madison wrote Jared Sparks about the convention's struggles with the issue of state representation in the Senate. He described the situation in the convention as "critical" and the issue as "the Gordian one." Both sides, he said, had shown "great zeal and pertinacity." Repeated tie votes prolonged the debates, and the situation became "not only distressing but seriously alarming." During this "period of gloom," said Madison, "Dr. Franklin made the proposition for a religious service in the Convention, an account of which was so erroneously given, with every semblance of authenticity, through the *National Intelligencer*, several years ago" (Farrand 1966, 3:498).

Three years later Madison again reviewed the background of Franklin's appeal for prayer, this time in response to an inquiry and a pamphlet by Thomas S. Grimke (Farrand 1966, 3:531). Madison wrote that Franklin's motion was treated with due respect and referred "to a highly respectable committee." As to the substance of the *National Intelligencer* article, Madison brusquely summarized, "That the communication was erroneous is certain; whether from misapprehension or misrecollection, uncertain."

Although the general tenor of the Dayton-Steele report exhibits some elements of verisimilitude, serious doubts must be expressed regarding many of its most crucial details. The long delay in making it public, the confusion in the sequence of events, the repeated references to the presence of a Rhode Island delegation, the unsupported assertion that morning prayers were instituted at the convention, the obvious attempt to damage Hamilton's posthumous reputation, the reference to Hamilton's wholly uncharacteristic discourtesy, and the highly homiletic tone of the Steele letter combine to make one prefer Madison's more nearly contemporary on-the-spot account.

When the entire record about Franklin's prayer proposal is reviewed, many questions remain unanswered. The motion had no observable effect, direct or indirect, on the government of the United States. It seems to have created no precedent for the practice of daily prayers in both Houses of Congress. The agreement of the states on a Constitution of the United States and its subsequent ratification by each of the State conventions, may have required, or at least involved, the kindly intervention of Providence. Even so, the Union was consummated without benefit of clergy.

Franklin's motivation remains in part a matter of speculation. Could an old man, to gain time, and perceiving catastrophic danger in the possible angry dissolution of the convention, have seized on prayer as a desperate temporary diversion? Given Franklin's determination to achieve a more effective system of national government, the old man *could* have done just that. Whether he was so motivated seems probable but not certain.

The proposal was, in fact, a diversion, deliberate or not, from the fierce and prolonged controversy, and was unrelated to the provisions of the Constitution itself.

However, recognition of Franklin's tactical shrewdness should not obscure his deeply held convictions regarding the social utility of religion. As a youth in Boston he had learned well the lessons of Puritan morality. Although he later rejected his father's sectarian theology, his moral standards remained. Franklin never supposed that a bad man could be a good politician (Ketcham 1965, xxviii).

Franklin's personal beliefs as to the value of prayer are not readily estimated. They were, at times and in some respects, mutually inconsistent. In youth he was so uncertain about the efficacy of prayer that in a span of five years he produced two essays, each arguing opposite sides of the question. Then, "the great uncertainty I found in Metaphysical reasonings disgusted me and I quitted that kind of reading and study."

It is probably significant that Cotton Mather's club in Boston was formed to promote religion whereas Franklin's *Junto* in Philadelphia sought to improve its members and the community where they lived (Fleming 1972, 59).

For sectarianism, Franklin clearly had no use. He regularly ridiculed its excesses. He even gave up church attendance when the sermons, for five successive Sundays, were "chiefly polemic Arguments, or explications of the peculiar Doctrines of our Sect . . . uninteresting and unedifying . . . not a single moral Principle was inculcated" (Lemay and Zoll 1986, 66). Franklin was "disgusted . . . and went no more to the public Assemblies."

Still, he took seriously the "little Liturgy" he wrote for his private use. His daily plan for moral perfection included a morning address to "Powerful Goodness." Furthermore he felt that Church and prayer were good for children and urged his daughter, "go constantly to Church whoever preaches, use the Book of Common Prayer," and "never miss the Prayer Days" (Fleming 1972, 184).

Did the Constitution prosper under God because Franklin piously urged daily prayers? Or, was it weakened by the failure of the convention to conduct such devotions? These are issues for theologians to ponder. Robert Morris, a Philadelphia delegate, summarized the events with a first-hand observation:

> Some have boasted the Constitution as a work from Heaven; others have given it a less righteous origin. I have many reasons to believe it is the work of plain honest men.

30 JUNE (SATURDAY)   Franklin again appealed for compromise, citing a carpenter who makes two boards fit snugly by taking a little off each of the two abutting sides (appendix A4). He concluded by reading a suggested compromise: equal votes for each state in the Senate and representation on money matters in the

House proportionate to each state's contribution to the national government's revenues. He put this proposition "on the table for consideration." No action was taken on his suggestion but his proposal for some sort of compromise bore fruit at the convention's next meeting.

2 JULY (MONDAY)   Disagreement on the representation issue now threatened to end the convention in stalemate and failure. The effort to ease the situation by the discussion of daily prayers may have been effective, but it was temporary. Perhaps Gouverneur Morris still had in mind Franklin's call-to-prayer of the preceding Thursday. He said, in a long discussion of oligarchy and democracy, "Reason tells us that we are but men, and we are not to expect any particular interference of Heaven in our favor" (Madison 1966, 234).

The basic issue remained. There were too many personal opinions, too many voices, too many choices. At this point, General Pinckney took the floor to endorse Franklin's recommendation for compromise, as made the preceding Saturday. Pinckney then formally proposed that the issue of equal *versus* proportional representation be referred to a committee of one member from each state to devise and report a compromise. After extended debate, on the general question to commit, the vote was 9-2 in favor, Pennsylvania voting aye.

On the question of composing the committee with "a member from each State," the vote was 10-1 in favor, Pennsylvania alone for some reason voting nay. The Madison *Notes* contain no explanation for the Pennsylvania delegation's mutability.

The following committee was then "elected by ballot":
Elbridge Gerry (Massachusetts)
Oliver Ellsworth (Connecticut)
Robert Yates (New York)
William Paterson (New Jersey)
Benjamin Franklin (Pennsylvania)
Gunning Bedford (Delaware)
Luther Martin (Maryland)
George Mason (Virginia)
William Davie (North Carolina)
John Rutledge (South Carolina)
Abraham Baldwin (Georgia)

One historian has observed that the committee membership included no outstanding spokesman for the nationalist viewpoint. Pennsylvania, he wrote, seemed to prefer the "kindly humor of the accommodating Franklin" to the vigorous legal advocacy of James Wilson (McLaughlin 1967, 234).

The National Park Service historians (Historians 1987, 66) also note the selection of Franklin, "old and ill," as they put it. Pennsylvania, they also observe, had available several "vigorous, young, articulate members,"—such as James Wilson and Gouverneur Morris.

At the same time, committee members from the small states were generally drawn from the least amenable delegates—Luther Martin of Maryland rather than Daniel Jenifer; Gunning Bedford of Delaware rather than George Read.

It was also voted "that time might be given the Committee, and to such as chose to attend the celebration of the Anniversary of Independence, the Convention adjourn until Thursday," July 5.

That evening Franklin invited a number of key delegates to a private dinner at his home. It seems unlikely that, at such a critical juncture, Franklin's motives were exclusively hospitable.

Another event of that disquieting day was the arrival of a memorial from the Pennsylvania Abolition Society asking the Convention to suppress the slave trade. Franklin was the recently elected President of that Society but the memorial was probably drafted by Tench Coxe, its secretary.[3]

In the tense controversy over representation another divisive issue might fatally impair the unity necessary even to continue the convention. Franklin suggested that debate on the memorial be postponed (Morris 1987, 183; Morris 1985, 193).

The convention considered the slave trade two months later, 25 August (see chapter 11).

3 JULY (TUESDAY) Franklin and the other ten members of the "Grand Committee" met at the State House. Elbridge Gerry was named chairman.

Some of the more industrious delegates, although not members of the committee, attended as observers. Among them was no less commanding a personage than General Washington, president of the convention. He was wearing that day his full-dress Continental Army uniform, blue and buff, with epaulets and three gold stars. He was thus attired not because it was the eve of Independence Day but because, after an early morning ride, he had come directly from a sitting for a portrait by Charles Willson Peale. The Philadelphia artist was painting his sixth portrait of the national hero.

After a repetition of the earlier debates on representation, the committee began to shape the compromise that they had been appointed to try to produce (Peters 1987, 100).

4 JULY (WEDNESDAY)   Independence Day recess came amid a six-day spell of hot weather (Farrand 1966, 3:554). The delegates could attend orations in the churches, toasts in the taverns, salvos on shipboard, fife and drum parades in the streets, and illuminations in the night sky. As delegates they had nothing to celebrate except another precarious year of national independence.

One of the public orators of the day assured the delegates that, although the nation was looking to them "with anxious speculation" and the existing plan of government had been fashioned "with a bayonet at our breasts and in the infancy of our knowledge of government," they were competent to form a better constitution (Warren 1967, 267).

5 JULY (THURSDAY)   The Committee on Compromise reported. Madison went out of his way to insert in his *Notes,* the following footnote:

"This report was founded on a motion in the Committee made by Dr. Franklin. . . ."

The *Notes* do not further describe Franklin's motion in the committee. It was not the committee report; it was the *basis* for the report. Possibly his motion was a broad statement of the necessity for agreement by compromise. Its content developed from discussion among several delegates including not only Franklin but also Judge Ellsworth, Roger Sherman, and John Dickinson.

Such a footnote is rare in the *Notes.* Possibly it was inserted to credit Franklin with his role in the achievement of compromise under difficult circumstances. Or, in view of Madison's steadfast disapproval of the one-state-one-vote principle in either Senate or House, the footnote may have been intended to fix on Franklin some of the responsibility for any adverse results of the compromise.

The text of the committee report follows:

I. That in the First branch of the Legislature each of the States now in the Union shall be allowed one member for every 40,000 inhabitants of the description reported in the seventh Resolution of the Committee of the Whole House; that each State not containing that number shall be allowed one member; that all bills for raising or appropriating money, and for fixing the Salaries of the officers of the Government of the United States shall originate in the first branch of the Legislature, and shall not be altered or amended by the second branch; and that no money shall be drawn from the public Treasury but in pursuance of appropriations to be originated in the first branch.

II. That in the second branch each State shall have an equal vote. (Madison 1966, 5 July, 237–38)

The committee shrewdly reported the two recommendations to the convention, *"on condition that both be generally adopted."*

Another special committee with different membership was named to propose the precise number of delegates for each state in the House of Representatives.

6 JULY (FRIDAY) When a motion was offered to allow Senate representation to be considered separately, Franklin insisted that the two parts of the report be considered together, "as mutual conditions of each other" (Madison 1966, 248).

Later that day, Franklin spoke in support of the requirement that legislation regarding money and salaries be required to originate in the House of Representatives (appendix B5).

9 JULY (MONDAY) Part 2 of Thursday's committee report was approved by the convention without further debate. However the number of members in the House was still unsatisfactory and the convention referred the question to yet another special committee for further study.

10 JULY (TUESDAY) The special committee recommended an increase in the House of Representatives from 56 to 65 (Farrand 1921, 101).

Two of the three New York delegates left the convention after their efforts to amend the report of the Compromise Committee were defeated.

The weather continued to be very hot, not conducive to equable tempers or a spirit of compromise. William Paterson of New Brunswick, New Jersey, wrote his wife that Philadelphia was "the warmest place I have been in."

13 JULY (FRIDAY) Manasseh Cutler of Massachusetts, not a delegate but a visitor in Philadelphia, was taken by Elbridge Gerry to call at Benjamin Franklin's residence. Cutler found himself in the midst of an informal gathering of men and women drinking tea in Franklin's garden. As it grew dark the men, most of whom were delegates, moved upstairs into Franklin's book-lined study. The conversation was wide-ranging, lasted until about 10 p.m., and had many references to botany and other sciences. The delegates were not supposed, under the secrecy rule, to discuss the content of the debate in the presence of an outside visitor such as Cutler, but it would be remarkable if some of them did not exchange a

few words privately about the recent debates in the Constitutional
Convention (Bowen 19?, 183; Van Doren, 1938, 750–71). Cutler
described Franklin as "a short, fat, trunched [stocky, squat] old
man in a plain Quaker dress, bald pate, and short white locks." He
also recalled that Franklin was affable, courteous, and in great
good humor. The weather on Friday was cooler (Farrand 1966,
3:554).

14 JULY (SATURDAY)   With cooler weather, a group of delegates
organized a 6 A.M. excursion. Beyond the Schuylkill ferry, they
explored William Bartram's Gardens surrounding a large old
stone house by the riverside. There they saw, among other unusual plants, some specimens of the rare *Franklinia alatamaha*.
Bartram's father, a respected working botanist, had found this
fragrant, silky-budded, white-flowered tree in the sandy bogs of
eastern Georgia some twenty years earlier. He brought its seeds or
seedlings home in his bulging saddle bags and named it in honor
of the president of the American Philosophical Society, his "be-
loved friend." At that season, *Franklinia* would be in bud but
probably not quite in full bloom.

After a 9:30 breakfast the delegates returned to the convention
where the debate on representation ground along all day without
reaching a decision.

The excursion included Cutler, Madison, Mason, Hamilton and
some others but it is very doubtful whether Franklin went along.
He had been up late the night before and the carriage ride might
have been painful. He had surely seen before the famous gardens
and the flowering, thirty-foot trees that bore his name.

16 JULY (MONDAY)   The ten states[4] in attendance at last adopted
the compromise by a vote of five to four, with the Massachusetts
delegation equally divided and therefore not counted—a very
close call!

Looking back over the busy month that elapsed between the
discussion of the New Jersey alternative for the Virginia Plan and
the adoption of the Great Compromise, Franklin had spoken
twice in the convention to support consultation instead of con-
frontation and mutual adjustments instead of division, had been
elected to the Committee on Compromise, had met with that
committee, had proposed the compromise embodied in its two
recommendations, and had insisted that both be adopted or rejected as one package.

Now he could turn, with other delegates, to consider other
issues still to be settled.

11
Chronology: Other Issues

1787

18 JULY (WEDNESDAY) Franklin supported a proposal by Gouverneur Morris to let judges' salaries be increased while they are in office. He said money may become more plentiful, or the judges' work may increase as population grows. (The proposal was adopted, 6-2.)

At tea that day, Franklin again found time to assist Noah Webster, who was copying excerpts from a history of New Jersey in Franklin's library. The book was probably related to Franklin's service as the New Jersey colonial printer in 1734 or as London agent for the colony in 1769 (Historians 1987, 88).

By this time Webster was as deeply involved in the convention as any nondelegate could be. He had been taught at Yale to regard liberty and union as two sides of the same coin (Babbidge 1967, 5). He had in 1786 toured the cities from Charleston to Portsmouth, partly to promote his new speller and partly to urge a strong central government in a continental union. He met the men of influence at every stop. At Mount Vernon he gave Washington a copy of his "Sketches of American Policy," had dinner, played whist, and spent the night. Webster came to believe, not without reason, that in some degree his writings and lectures helped bring about the convention and the resulting Constitution. He supported himself as a visiting teacher of language and mathematics at the Philadelphia Episcopal Academy but made time to meet often with Franklin, Washington, Madison, King, Sherman, Randolph, Johnson, Ellsworth, and other "Convention gentlemen" (Warfel 1936, 166).

20 JULY (FRIDAY) Franklin spoke in defense of a clause making executive officers impeachable (appendix B6). Provisions to that effect were included in the Constitution.

Franklin's views on impeachment were widely shared. The convention's most outspoken and influential members evinced a deep

107

fear of executive power. Thus Gerry opposed popular election of a president because "if he is so chosen and does his duty he will be thrown out of office" (Madison 1966, 337–39). The equally cynical Mason reasoned "from the nature of man" that those who have power will not give it up and Madison concluded that "all men having power ought to be distrusted" (Madison 1966, 226, 272).

23 JULY (MONDAY)   The number of senators per state was considered. It was agreed by a 9-1 vote that each senator would vote independently rather than as part of a state delegation. That procedure being settled, there was no need to have an odd number of senators from each state to avoid immobilizing an entire delegation. Morris, however, suggested three senators per state, Gorham suggested two. All were aware that other states would soon be added to the original thirteen.

Gorham predicted that Kentucky, Vermont, Maine, and Franklin (eventually named Tennessee[1]), and perhaps others, should be expected (Madison 1966, 354). This prospect tended to minimize the number of senators per state to limit the total size of the Senate. At last, two senators per state was approved without opposition (Farrand 1921, 135–36).

26 JULY (THURSDAY)   Franklin, supporting Mason's motion for a seven-year term, told the convention that the president should be ineligible for a second term. Since the people are sovereign in a republic, he argued, the return of an elected leader to private life should rightly be regarded as a promotion (appendix B7).

Later that day, cynical Gouverneur Morris responded with irony to Franklin by saying, "I have no doubt that our Executive, like most others, would have too much patriotism to shrink from the burden of his office, and too much modesty not to be willing to decline the promotion" (Madison 1966, 371–72).

The convention elected a five-man Committee on Detail to "arrange and systematize" the material thus far approved. The convention then adjourned for ten days to give the committee time to work (Van Doren 1943, 138).

31 JULY (TUESDAY)   The presiding officer, George Washington, not being needed for the small Committee on Detail, used part of the recess to visit nearby Valley Forge where, ten years earlier, 11,000 men under his command had suffered, sickened, shivered, and starved to win American independence.

4 AUGUST (SATURDAY)   The convention being still in recess to await the report of the Committee of Detail, Noah Webster called on the two busiest delegates—Madison and Franklin.

When Webster in 1789 published his *Dissertations on the English Language,* he appropriately dedicated the great work "to his Excellency, Benjamin Franklin, Esq., LL.D., F.R.S., late President of the Commonwealth of Pennsylvania," with four pages of encomium.[2]

Their shared interest in language was as much patriotic as it was linguistic. Webster believed that the difference between English and "Federal" (as he called it) was "an object of vast political consequence." Besides, "a national language is a band of national union" (quoted in Mencken 1957, 382). Indeed, their discussions of language as an aspect of government foreshadowed modern debates about bilingual instruction and English as the official language.

The Franklin who had developed his first plans for continental unity in 1752 and 1754 and was now helping to produce a plan for Federation could find young Webster's concerns entirely relevant to the purposes of the Constitutional Convention.

In the next few weeks a plan was developed to employ young Webster's talents more directly. On 15 September, Pennsylvania delegate Thomas Fitzsimmons, possibly acting on Franklin's suggestion, wrote Webster that he might be "eminently useful" in developing public support for the Constitution, then nearly completed. Webster eagerly complied. In two days he drafted *The Leading Principles of the Federal Constitution Proposed by the Late Convention in Philadelphia.* He began with a lavish tribute to the framers, comparing them to the Jewish law-givers at Sinai and "the fabled demigods of antiquity." His analysis of the Constitution, though lacking the arid logic of the *Federalist,* supported the national government with persuasive eloquence (Babbidge 1967, 58).

7 AUGUST (TUESDAY) The city and the state in the morning welcomed some eight hundred officers and enlisted men of the state militia just returned from the service of the United States on the northwest frontier at Forts Harmar and Vincennes. These troops made their reports to President Benjamin Franklin and the State Supreme Executive Council before they were mustered out.

Later that same day, as it happened, Franklin delivered in the convention his unrehearsed tribute to "the public spirit of our common people." He strenuously opposed a proposal by Gouverneur Morris to limit the suffrage to freeholders (appendix B8). Madison later said of Franklin: "Humbly born, but by all odds the man of greatest worldly experience in the country, he from time to time expressed his dislike of every thing that tended to debase the common people." The Morris motion was defeated, 1-7.

The importance of this decision is emphasized by its deviation from past requirements. The established policy of colonial and early national elections held that only property owners should vote or seek office. Property, in this context, meant real estate. The Northwest Ordinance, for instance, provided for a landed oligarchy:

> "No person shall be eligible or qualified to act as representative unless he . . . shall hold in his own right in fee simple two hundred acres of land . . . provided also that a freehold in fifty acres of land in the district shall be necessary to qualify a man as an elector of a representative" (quoted by Rohrbaugh in Sheehan 1987, 55).

The Morris amendment divided the convention sharply and split two of the most powerful state delegations—Pennsylvania and Virginia.

When Franklin took the floor in opposition he did not have his usual neatly written speech, prepared in advance with a copy for Madison's files. Nor did he ask any other delegate to stand or speak for him. He reminded the Convention that American seamen, captured and thrust into British prisons, had refused to gain their freedom and make their fortunes by serving on British naval vessels. Captured British seamen, however, readily served on American ships. Franklin attributed the difference to the different treatment accorded to the ordinary citizens.

9 AUGUST (THURSDAY) Franklin repeated that the origin of money bills in the House and the equality of state representation in the Senate were "essentially connected" by the agreed report of the Committee on Compromise.

Franklin said that foreigners should not be required to live in the United States for as long as fourteen years before becoming eligible for public office (appendix B9). Many aliens, he said, had served the United States faithfully during the revolution. When our many friends in Europe, pursuing a chance for greater happiness, give their preference to our country, he said, we should receive them with confidence and affection.

His policy, as applied to only nine years of citizenship before eligibility to the Senate, was then adopted, 6-4, with North Carolina divided and so not counted.

10 AUGUST (FRIDAY) Charles Pinckney tried again to set property ownership as a requirement for the executive, the courts, and the Congress. He proposed that persons chosen for these positions be required to swear that they owned "clear and unencumbered estates." The motion suggested, in the case of the president, an

estate worth at least $100,000 and lesser estates for the other offices.

Franklin opposed the measure on principle. Said Franklin, "If honesty is often the companion of wealth, and if poverty is exposed to peculiar temptation, it is not less true that the possession of property increases the desire for more property." Some of the greatest rogues he ever knew, he declared, were the richest rogues. He mentioned the scriptural injunction that rulers "should be men hating coveteousness"[3] (appendix B10).

Franklin stood to deliver this speech extemporaneously and in person, as he did for the similar defense of the common people on August 7. When he finished, the opposition to Pinckney's proposal was so evident that it was not even put to a vote (Van Doren 1943, 143).

Rossiter, although he found Franklin at times "a purveyor of irrelevant information," believed that Franklin's "greatest rogues" speech of 10 August was one of the "finest moments" of the summer (Rossiter 1968, 181, 212).

13 AUGUST (MONDAY)   Washington "took tea" at Franklin's house with Franklin and his daughter, Sarah Bache.[4]

20 AUGUST (MONDAY)   Franklin supported, in the clause on treason, a requirement of two witnesses to the same overt act for a conviction. "Prosecutions against treason," he said, "are generally virulent and perjury too easily made use of against innocence." The requirement was approved, 8-3, and the Constitution (Article 3, Section 3) contains such protective provisions.

Franklin had good reason to be sensitive on the topic of treason.

In London, amid British indignation over the Boston Tea Party, he believed he might be prosecuted for treason by distortion of the meaning of some of his letters. Franklin knew that under English law treason was a grievous capital offense. He knew that the savage penalties upon conviction included, in addition to a dishonorable public execution, forfeiture of all real property to the Crown and "Corruption of Blood," a legal term that forbade the convicted person to inherit, keep, or transmit any estate or title he possessed. In the United States this penalty was expressly forbidden by Article 3, Section 3, of the Constitution.

Franklin felt keenly the injustice of this threat, partly because he was offering to pay personally for the destroyed tea if the punitive measures against Massachusetts were repealed, and partly because, "Much Violence must be us'd with my Letters before they can be construed into Treason."

Nevertheless, Lord Sandwich in the House of Lords, looking straight at Franklin, called him Britain's "most mischievous enemy," while the Earl of Hillsborough in the same forum declared that Franklin should either be placed in the Middlesex County Gaol at Newgate or on the gallows at Tyburn (Fleming 1972, 44, 59; Van Doren 1938, 414, 512; McDonald 1988, 10).

21 AUGUST (TUESDAY)   John Fitch, a young clockmaker from nearby Bucks County, demonstrated his new "steam boat" for the convention delegates. Six steam-driven oars on each side propelled the vessel canoe-style, by alternately striking the water on port and starboard. Some of the delegates risked an excursion, steaming down the Delaware and up the Schuylkill. Fitch, who had previously called on Franklin, said he believed his invention had a bright future. However Franklin was not impressed. He did not examine the boat and would not take the excursion "mostly because of the difficulty of getting there." Granting the technical possibility of steam propulsion, Franklin continued to doubt its economic feasibility (Ford 1946, 12; Warren 1967, 511–12). Meanwhile, at the convention the remaining[5] delegates discussed the national debt, taxation, and the slave trade (Madison 1966, 494–503).

25 AUGUST (SATURDAY)   The Convention extended the slave trade to 1807. As on many other important constitutional issues, no convention records show Franklin's personal position on slavery. However, he voted with the rest of the Pennsylvania delegation to halt the slave trade. When that proposal was rejected he understood that acquiescence was the price of union (McCaughey 1987, 59).

Other records show that for thirty years he expounded the inhumanity and the economic inefficiency of the slave trade. "Slaves," he told the Second Continental Congress, "rather weaken than strengthen the state."

In 1758, observing that the free blacks in Pennsylvania, although poor, uneducated, and improvident, were "not deficient in natural understanding," he supported the state's first free school for blacks.

By 1787 Franklin's continued concern culminated in his presidency of "The Pennsylvania Society for Promoting the Abolition of Slavery and the Relief of Free Negroes Unlawfully Held in Bondage."

After the convention, Franklin signed, and may have written (Van Doren 1938, 774), the Society's "Address to the Public" appealing for funds and support. He also signed the society's memorial to the first Congress under the new Constitution. When a congressional committee in March 1790 reported the Congress had no jurisdiction in the matter, Franklin, with less than a month to live, wrote and published his devastating response, a brilliant satire "On the Slave Trade." That essay cleverly "quoted," with stinging derision, an imaginary Muslim, living a century earlier and using precisely the arguments of the current apologists for slavery to justify the Algerians in holding captured Christians as their slaves.

3 SEPTEMBER (MONDAY)   Washington visited Franklin (Jackson 1976–79, 5:183). It was the fourth anniversary of the Treaty of Paris, ending the Revolutionary War.

They may have remembered the anniversary, but they probably did not spend much time reminiscing. Their attention was directed to "a Machine called a Mangle for pressing, in place of Ironing, clothes from the wash." Washington gravely concluded that, for "such Articles as have not pleats," and in large families, a Mangle would be "very useful." After delivering that opinion Washington went home for dinner and the evening at the Robert Morris's (Historians 1987, 168).

7 SEPTEMBER (FRIDAY)   Franklin seconded Mason's motion to create a council of state for the chief executive (appendix B11). Although supported also by Madison, Dickinson, and Wilson, the proposal was rejected, 3-8. It was agreed, however, that the president could call on heads of departments for their opinions in writing (Farrand 1913, 171–72).

8 SEPTEMBER (SATURDAY)   A Committee on Style was appointed "to revise the style of and arrange the articles." The members were Johnson, Hamilton, Gouverneur Morris, Madison, and King. This committee phrased the Preamble beginning "We, the People. . .," a phrase which, although impossible at the outset of the convention, was accepted without question at the end. The convention had met to revise the Articles of Confederation; it ended by framing an entirely new instrument, the Constitution of the United States (Farrand 1921, 190–91).

10 SEPTEMBER (MONDAY)   Late in the session Governor Edmund Randolph, a delegate from Virginia, recited a long list of objections to the Constitution. They ranged all the way from lack of controls over Congress in fixing its own pay to inadequate limits on the presidential power to grant pardons. He then predicted that its adoption would lead to tyranny. He moved that the document be sent first to the Continental Congress, next to the state

legislatures, and finally to another general convention. In essence, he proposed to start all over again.

Franklin seconded this motion without other recorded comment. Mason and Pinckney, however, got the motion tabled and the session adjourned without action on it.

Franklin's reasons for seconding Randolph's motion are unknown. It was a strange move for "a man of such experience and wisdom" (Rossiter 1968, 114).

He may have noticed that earlier in the day Randolph candidly admitted that he did not expect his proposal to win approval. He said he would offer it only to discharge his duty and "give quiet to his own mind." Franklin may therefore have reflected that with a little harmless encouragement Randolph might yet be won over to support the Constitution as the best available solution. Support from the governor would be a substantial advantage in securing ratification by Virginia.

By that time, all the delegates must have seen that the convention was moving swiftly to its end. Some clarifications were still needed, some administrative matters remained to be handled, and a supreme effort must be exerted to end on a statement as near to unanimity as possible. Franklin began to formulate such a statement. He would have it ready to read before the final vote on the final day.

12
Chronology: Decision and Epilogue

1787

12 SEPTEMBER (WEDNESDAY) The Committee on Style reported a text of a draft Constitution as well as a transmittal letter to the Congress. Madison's *Notes* (1966, 616) do not explain the origins of this letter. However, the convention secretary, Major Jackson, writing in 1818 to John Quincy Adams, found it "almost impossible in the lapse of thirty years to state occurrences with accuracy." He was "inclined to believe," however, that on 17 September a committee of three Pennsylvania delegates—Franklin, Gouverneur Morris, and Jared Ingersoll—had drafted the letter for Washington's signature. As to the date, the major's memory was faulty, but he may have been right about the composition of the drafting committee. His *Journal* records only that the letter was agreed to by the convention, paragraph by paragraph (Farrand 1966, 4:83).

The letter is brisk, respectful, and optimistic. The prose seems as much in the style of Morris as in that of Franklin. The substance, however, reflects both Franklin's opinions and his self-deprecatory approach. The Constitution is not offered as perfect but as "most adviseable." Individuals must "give up a share of liberty to preserve the rest." The letter concludes with the same theme as Franklin's conciliatory speech of 17 September—the Constitution "is liable to as few exceptions as could reasonably be expected" (Madison 1966, 626).

Washington that afternoon "dined with the President," which in context means with Franklin. Washington's diary mentions no other guests. In this final week of the convention it would have been natural for old friends to review the status of political affairs—and the future outlook.

Abraham Baldwin and perhaps other delegates also came to that dinner. The topics of discussion are not known but, with convention adjournment less than a week ahead, it is quite sure that efforts were in progress to ensure the affirmative votes of doubtful delegates. Baldwin, thirty-three years old, had recently moved to Georgia from Connecticut. He had been a Georgia delegate to Congress in New York City with special responsibility for overseeing state accounts.

It may also be noted that Baldwin was very active in establishing higher education in Georgia. In 1785 the forerunner of the present state university had been hopefully chartered. It began operations in Athens, Georgia, in 1801. The trustees in 1806 with evident pride named their first building there "Franklin College, after Benjamin Franklin." The institution was ordinarily and officially called by that name at least as late as 1839.

The new building was appropriately equipped with several lightning rods. The Trustees also insured it prudently with the Phoenix Company of London (Dyer 1985, 7, 24, 41; Historians 1987, 183).

13 SEPTEMBER (THURSDAY)   Franklin was appointed to a convention committee to report on how delegates could by their "advice, influence, and example" encourage "economy, frugality, and American manufactures." The motion to create the committee was made by Mason and seconded by Johnson, both of whom were also named to the committee of five members, along with Dickinson of Delaware and Livingston of New Jersey.

One may safely assume that the delegates knew the Convention was drawing to its close and that the likelihood of either a meeting of the committee or of a formal report by it, was exceedingly remote. One may also be sure that no one wished to weaken Mason's fragile support for the Constitution by opposing his wishes on a procedural matter.

14 SEPTEMBER (FRIDAY)   Franklin moved to add a few words to empower Congress "to provide for cutting canals where deemed necessary" (Madison 1966, 14 September 638–39).

Wilson seconded this motion. Sherman objected that the expense would be met by the United States but benefits would apply only to the places along the canals. Madison proposed a wider power to enable Congress "to grant charters of incorporation where the interest of the United States might require and legislative provisions of individual states would be incompetent." Randolph seconded the Madison motion. King thought the power unnecessary. Wilson retorted that it *is* necessary to prevent a *state* from obstructing the *general* welfare. The two men exchanged words again on the broader implications of the Madison motion.

Mason suggested limiting the issue only to the original question—canals. On that basis the question was put and defeated 8-3. Pennsylvania, Virginia, and Georgia supported Franklin's canal proposal.

With only one more working day, Friday was not a good time for action on apparently novel ideas, however worthy. Other rejected suggestions that day included proposals by Madison and Pinckney to establish a national university, by Mason and Randolph forbidding standing armies in peacetime, and by Pinckney and Gerry to proclaim the liberty of the press. All were declared unnecessary or unwise and were buried in the rush to complete the drafting.

Because of their long friendship, Franklin surely knew that Washington, although silent as usual in the chair, attached great importance to public support for canals. Indeed, it is not impossible that Franklin offered his amendments on Washington's behalf as a sequel to their private talks over dinner at Franklin's house two days earlier.

Washington, in his youthful days of surveys and campaigns, saw that Cumberland Gap could be linked to Tidewater Virginia by canals around Great Falls. After inspecting his western lands in 1784 he also believed the Potomac waterway might be extended all the way to Lake Erie. He told General Knox that western settlements, unless given easy access to Eastern markets, could become separate, powerful, and dangerous neighbors. On the other hand he viewed "the vast inland navigation of the United States" as a basis for "a new Empire." Inland navigation was thus a magnet strong enough to draw a reluctant, retired general at Mount Vernon into public life again (Taylor 1987, 12).

Franklin himself had been interested in canals for years. They might be useful in the Postal Service and in helping to develop national cohesion. In 1772 Franklin wrote, "Rivers are ungovernable things, especially in hilly Countries, but Canals are quiet and very manageable" (Clark 1985, 96). Indeed, in his raw, sprawling land, better transport assumed a patriotic tinge (Farrand 1921, 28).

Defeat of his canal proposal had historic consequences. In 1811 Gouverneur Morris, then chairman of the Erie Canal Commission, and DeWitt Clinton, governor of New York, jointly asked Congress for funds to finance the Erie Canal between Albany and Buffalo. The request was denied. New York State in 1825, after eight years of construction, completed the major new waterway with its own resources, at a cost of $7 million (Miers 1956, 128).

Madison, as late as 1831, still recalled the convention debates about Franklin's proposal, and maintained that power to build canals "would have been properly vested in Congress." He ascribed the rejection to fears that adoption might increase the difficulties of securing state ratification (Farrand 1966, 32:494–95).

15 SEPTEMBER (SATURDAY)   Rutledge and Franklin jointly moved to add to Article 2 the following: "and he [the president] shall not receive within that period any other emolument from the United States or any of them" (Madison 1966, 15 September, 645). The vote was 7-3 in favor. Thus Franklin, who did not think the president should be paid any salary at all, at least moved a little nearer to his goal by denying any emolument other than salary.

The convention voted 6-4 that it would not publish an "Address to the People," but would send its recommendations to the Congress with a letter of transmittal.

To complete its work the convention remained in session until six that evening. Madison noted that on the question to agree to the Constitution, as amended, all the states voted in the affirmative. The Constitution was ordered to be engrossed and thus prepared for formal signing (Farrand 1913, 191).

16 SEPTEMBER (SUNDAY)   The penman must have worked on the Sabbath, the Fourth Commandment notwithstanding, to prepare a clean copy of the four-page parchment document. So, in all likelihood, did the printers who ran off 500 copies as ordered.

These artisans were not the only people in Philadelphia who were at work that Sunday. Benjamin Franklin summoned the Pennsylvania delegates to meet at his home. Rumors circulated that Franklin called the unusual Sunday meeting to inform the other Pennsylvania delegates that he intended to denounce the document, indicating the points they could not possibly accept. In fact, as an unknown informant wrote to Jefferson in Paris, Franklin told his colleagues that he wanted them to help "allay every possible scruple and make their votes unanimous." Jefferson's correspondent, writing him from Philadelphia soon after the convention adjourned, concluded that "Dr. Franklin has gained much credit within doors [i.e., among insiders] for his conduct" (Farrand 1966, 3:104–5).

In Philadelphia, Franklin had already written his final speech, ready for delivery the next day.

17 SEPTEMBER (MONDAY)   Final day of the Constitutional Convention. The Constitution of the United States had been prepared

for signatures. The early autumn weather had cooled again. The morning sun shone through the south windows of the meeting room. Benjamin Franklin, already reaching out to secure the largest possible number of affirmative votes and to arrange prompt ratification by the states, had written out a speech, which Wilson read for him (appendix A5).

> Sir, I agree to this Constitution with all its faults, if they are such, because I think a general government necessary. . . .

Franklin's motion that the Constitution be signed, "done in Convention by the unanimous consent of *the States* present," was drafted for him by Gouverneur Morris to enable some opponents to sign as part of a state from which the majority of delegates present had voted approval.

The speech in which Franklin invited each delegate to "doubt a little of his infallibility and . . . put his name to this instrument" was a powerful impetus for state ratification of the Constitution. And without state ratification, the whole weary process of the past four months would have been nullified. Franklin's short, persuasive, and quotable speech became "the literary masterpiece of the Convention." Delegates asked for copies to be used in their respective states. Franklin readily provided copies of the speech and permitted its publication for wider distribution (Van Doren 1938, 756).

After Franklin's speech and formal motion, a minor last-minute change was made in the text of Article 1, Section 2, increasing the maximum number of members in the House of Representatives from one for every forty thousand inhabitants to one for every thirty thousand. This proposal was supported by four delegates and adopted without objection.

At this point, according to Madison's *Notes* (1966, 655), the Constitution was "agreed to, all *the States* answering ay."

But the Convention was not yet quite over. Edmund Randolph of Virginia, who had opened the debate four months earlier, now took the floor. Apologetically referring to Franklin's appeal for unanimity, Randolph said he would not sign the Constitution, "notwithstanding the vast majority and venerable names that would give sanction to its wisdom and worth."

This announcement should not have been greatly surprising to Franklin and other convention delegates. The high probability that Randolph, his fellow Virginian George Mason, and Elbridge Gerry of Massachusetts would constitute a bloc of three nonsigners was already recognized.

Accepting this small minority vote was not easy, but a much greater danger was that others might augment the negative group. This peril had produced Morris's carefully worded motion and Franklin's appeal for unanimity. As Hamilton feared, "A few characters of consequence, by opposing, or even refusing to sign the Constitution might do infinite mischief."

Randolph pressed on with his explanation. Not signing, he said, did not mean that he would publicly oppose the Constitution, "without doors." He would be governed by judgments not yet reached. He feared, he said, the confusion that would surely ensue when, as he expected, nine States refused to ratify. If that happened, he concluded, "he ought not, he could not," pledge to support the plan.

Gouverneur Morris said that he, too, had objections but he would accept the Constitution as the best attainable. The alternative, he said firmly, was "a general anarchy."

Williamson, obviously trying to find something that every delegate could sign, said that he saw no prospect for a better plan and had no scruples against "putting his name to it." He nevertheless suggested that the only document they need all sign was the letter of transmittal placing the Constitution before the Continental Congress. This, he thought, would be satisfactory to his colleague from North Carolina William Blount, and to some other delegates who had objections to the Constitution.

As soon as he could get the floor, Blount spoke up for himself. He had, after all, served four years in the unhappy role of paymaster in the North Carolina military and he was no stranger to the claims of state sovereignty and of the national government. He said that, although he had already announced that he would not sign the Constitution, he was now ready to "attest the fact that the plan was the unanimous act of the States in Convention." This was William Blount's only recorded speech at the convention. He had attended in silence for forty-eight days, but his one remark on the last day was well-timed at almost the last moment. The latest convert is always doubly welcomed by the rejoicing congregation.

Franklin then took the floor again, this time without a prepared paper or a spokesman. He said:

> I fear from what Mr. Randolph has said, that he thinks I was alluding to him in my remarks this morning. When I drafted that paper I did not know that any particular member would refuse to sign. I hope that is understood. I feel a high sense of obligation to Mr. Randolph for bringing forward the plan in the first instance, and for

the assistance he has given in its progress. I hope that he will yet lay aside his objections and, by concurring with his brethren, prevent the great mischief which the refusal of his name might produce.

Despite this renewed plea, Randolph said the form of the motion was not important. Although refusal to sign was "a step which might be the most awful of his life," he feared "anarchy and civil convulsions" if the Constitution were presented for acceptance and rejection without any other choices. He could not hesitate, much less change. (He did, however, do both; when Virginia the following June considered the Constitution, Randolph supported ratification.)

Gerry now added to the tension. He, too, feared a "Civil War." In Massachusetts, he explained, there were two parties—"one devoted to Democracy, the worst of all possible evils, the other as violent in the opposite extreme." He would never sign, he said, but he respected the decision of the convention and would not make public his refusal to sign. Franklin's remarks, he said, were clearly leveled at himself and the other nonsigners.

Talk about signing a document without agreeing to support it began to irritate the senior delegate from South Carolina, General Pinckney. We shall win no converts, he said, by deliberate ambiguity. He intended to be candid. His purpose in the convention would not be served if the intention of the signers were left in doubt. As far as he was concerned, he would sign the Constitution then and there, and pledge himself to support it with all his influence.

Franklin now set a new record for himself in the frequency of speaking during a single session. Taking the floor a third time, and apparently fearing that Pinckney's emphatic support might give the impression that signing meant supporting, and thus provide other delegates an excuse not to sign, Franklin said courteously that it was too soon to *pledge* support (as if such a pledge were a prerequisite for signing). Our pledge of support, he said, could wait until the Continental Congress and the people have approved the plan. He clearly wished to end the meeting without more exchanges.

Jared Ingersoll of Pennsylvania, with the same obvious intention, said that signing was neither an attestation that every state supported the Constitution nor a pledge to support it whatever might happen. To sign was merely a recommendation that, all things considered, it was the most "eligible" or preferable text

(Madison 1966, 655–58). This timely support by Franklin's old friend was Ingersoll's only recorded comment in the convention (Historians 1987, 25). It was worth waiting for.

Franklin's motion, this time on a roll-call vote, was then adopted 10-0, with South Carolina divided and so not counted, presumably because some of its delegates did not feel the motion gave a sufficiently emphatic approval. All four delegates from the state signed the instrument nevertheless.

Now the signing began. According to one recently written history, "Franklin had to be helped slowly to the front of the room [to sign] and it was said that he wept as he signed" (Mee 1987, 280).

The states were arranged in geographical order to receive the signatures of the delegates. Thus it happens that the signature of the youngest delegate, Jonathon Dayton of New Jersey, stands next to that of the oldest delegate, placed at the head of the Pennsylvania delegation.

While one delegation after another was signing the document, Franklin managed one more vivid comment (appendix B12). "I have," he said, off the record, "often and often in the course of the session . . . looked at that behind the President" [i.e., at the sun painted on the back of the president's chair] "without being able to tell whether it was rising or setting. But now at length I have the happiness to know that it is a rising and not a setting sun."

Mrs. Samuel Powel, a prominent and well-to-do citizen, wife of the mayor of Philadelphia, was one of a small group waiting outside the door as the delegates left Independence Hall for the last time. Spotting a familiar figure in the group she called out, "Doctor, what have we got, a Republic or a Monarchy?"

To which Franklin, freed now by the adjournment to speak out, responded with a conditional warning, "A Republic, if you can keep it" (Farrand 1966, 3:85).

Those were probably the last words spoken about the Constitution by a delegate at the Convention Hall.

About six o'clock in the afternoon some of the delegates gathered at the City Tavern nearby for food, felicitations, and farewells.

18 SEPTEMBER   At 11 A.M. (the morning after!), the Pennsylvania delegation, led by Benjamin Franklin, came before a special session of the Pennsylvania State Assembly. Before the officially certified text could arrive at the meeting of the Congress in New York City, Franklin had the full text of the Constitution read aloud to the state assembly in Philadelphia. He reported triumphantly that the Constitutional Convention had completed its work and

that the proposed Constitution would "promote the happiness and prosperity of this Commonwealth . . . and of the United States."

Characteristically, Franklin's report was followed immediately by presenting a letter from the state delegation to secure for his state the honor (and profit) of providing the capital city of the United States of America. The delegation suggested that the legislature select and set aside a ten-mile-square tract for this purpose (Van Doren 1938, 742–56).

Franklin also began writing to friends in Philadelphia, England, France, and Italy, enclosing copies of the Constitution.

7 DECEMBER   Delaware ratified the Constitution, the first state to do so.

12 DECEMBER   Pennsylvania became the second state to ratify. However, Franklin did not sit in the Pennsylvania state ratification convention.

13 DECEMBER   Franklin, with other officers of the Pennsylvania government, proclaimed the ratification. A solemn little procession went to the courthouse where the Instrument of Ratification was read out to the public. (Van Doren 1943, 227–28).

1788

4 JULY   A combined celebration in Philadelphia of the Declaration of Independence and the Constitution was organized in a huge parade. About five thousand people marched in the three-hour procession. A copy of the Constitution was carried aloft through the streets. Decorated floats rattled past. They represented the Ship of State, the American eagle, and the "Foederal Republic" with its three unfinished columns representing New York, North Carolina, and Rhode Island. Salvos were fired by cannons on a ship moored in the harbor. The name of the saluting ship was *The Rising Sun*. Franklin's son-in-law, Richard Bache, was the herald of the procession. Major William Jackson commanded a troop of the Philadelphia Cavalry. Ten toasts were proposed at the public dinner afterwards. The first toast was: "The People of the United States."

Franklin may have glimpsed the parade from a window of his nearby house but by then he had become too frail to attend any part of the public celebration (Van Doren 1943, 297ff).

1789

20 APRIL   Washington rode up Philadelphia's flower-decked streets on his way to New York and the Presidency. At City Tavern he was entertained by fireworks at a dinner for 250 guests. Franklin, by that time, was confined to his room, his severe pain relieved by opiates, but still clear in mind and interested in public affairs.

28 APRIL   Washington reached New York for his inauguration, staying there at the Franklin Inn.

13

The Oldest Delegate

This is the record of a man in his eighties who, with colleagues averaging half his age, met daily for four months to exert what he must have known would be his final effort to perform a useful service to his country.

This chapter offers an appraisal of Franklin's part in the convention. After a summary of his health and age, it reviews all his recorded proposals (whether they were accepted, rejected, or ignored) and the main principles of government that motivated him.

HEALTH

Other discussions of Franklin's role in the federal convention usually begin, and almost invariably end, with age and frailty. Let us begin there; let us not end there.

BODILY INFIRMITIES

Evaluations of an old person rarely deal with character or competence. They begin, as a rule, with current ailments, go on to solicitous advice about medications, and end in gloomy counsels of resignation.

When one is young, the interest taken by others in one's health is usually perfunctory and descriptive; as one grows older that concern becomes intense and prognostic. At an advanced age good health may be regarded as an impudent challenge to the proper order of things.

Franklin while young enjoyed the bliss of being alive. Illness was a temporary and tolerable inconvenience. There was one exception: at age twenty-one pleurisy nearly killed him. Forty years later he could still recall his own sardonic regret, even as he recovered, that "I must now sometime or other have all that disagreeable work to do over again" (Lemay and Zoll 1986, 41).

Later he developed two chronic disabilities—gout and stone. Gout, which came at increasingly frequent intervals after 1765, seems to have been aggravated by stress. The kidney stone, which he first noticed in 1783, caused pain occasionally severe enough to be temporarily disabling (Clark 1983, 213, 385).

Still, as late as 1786, Franklin could assure Dr. Benjamin Rush that he "had not felt better in the last thirty years." If he inflicted descriptions of his indispositions on other delegates, none recorded the event. And, three days after the convention ended, Franklin informed his sister, Jane, "My health continues" (Aldridge 1965, 381).

Transient discomforts did not destroy Franklin's effectiveness. They did not cause him to be more often absent, or to play a role less active, than those of most of his junior colleagues.

THE SEDAN CHAIR

At some time during his last years, Franklin began occasional use of a sedan, a portable chair for one passenger. Enclosed with glass-paneled doors, it was carried on long poles by four or two bearers. Franklin joked that he sometimes wished to be transported by a balloon, but the sedan could reduce the discomforts of carriage travel on rough roads. Franklin's sedan chair, like almost everything else he owned, was a famous object of public curiosity.

There are so many substantial variants and ambiguities about Franklin's sedan that a separate note on the subject is added. In brief, he rarely used it, if at all, during the Convention. He routinely walked the short distance to the daily meetings. He may have used the sedan more often in later years.

MENTAL ALERTNESS

One may evaluate and review evidences of Franklin's physical infirmities but his mental acuity is scarcely open to doubt. The records of Madison and other contemporaries demonstrate that Franklin possessed an extraordinarily agile and probing mind— and that he used it regularly during the convention.

His convention colleague, William Pierce, for instance, reached the firm and somewhat startled conclusion that Franklin possessed "an activity of mind equal to a youth of 25 years" (Farrand 1966, 3:91).

Another observer came from outside the convention. Manasseh Cutler on Friday 13 July, had the good fortune to spend a pleasant evening with Franklin. He noted at once "the brightness of his memory, and the clearness and vivacity of all his mental faculties, *notwithstanding his age*" (emphasis added, Van Doren 1938, 751). Cutler, a well-educated scientist-clergyman-merchant, was delighted by his conversation with the old philosopher, by his "incessant vein of humor," and by his "unrestrained freedom of manners." These observations were not made on some ideal brisk, invigorating Autumn morning; they occurred on a warm mid-July night at about ten in the evening.

DOWNHILL, AFTERWARDS

After the convention, Franklin's health deteriorated markedly. One could suppose that he had garnered and expended all his remaining energies for one final effort on a great occasion. In 1788 a French observer reported to his government on some of the important delegates. Of Franklin, he wrote, "The philosopher who confronted the thunderbolts of the heavens and of the English Parliament will not struggle much longer against the infirmities of age. We must regret that immortality belongs only to his name and to his writings" (Farrand 1966, 3:235–36). In fact, Franklin survived just thirty-one months to the day after the Convention adjourned.

AGE

AT HOME IN THE WORLD

Great age makes other impacts beside the simple fact of longevity. His long life placed Franklin, more than most people, in several very different epochs and environments.

When he was born, the British Empire was ruled by Queen Anne, the rotund daughter of the last of the Stuarts.

When he was an apprentice, he knew the renowned Boston preacher, Cotton Mather, visited his home, read his books, and heard his fiery sermons.

When Franklin first visited London, the throne was occupied by

George I, great grandfather of the monarch who would learn to regard Franklin as the most dangerous man in America.

When Franklin became a successful Philadelphia printer, the colony of Georgia had not yet been founded.

Over the years, Franklin's long list of some four thousand accumulated correspondents, colleagues, and friends included, from Britain: Edmund Burke, James Boswell, David Garrick, Edward Gibbon, Lord Kames, William Pitt, Joseph Priestley, Adam Smith. From France: Beaumarchais, Condorcet, Houdon, Lafayette, Lavoisier, Mirabeau, Turgot, Voltaire. From America: John Adams, John Quincy Adams, John Hancock, John Jay, John Paul Jones, Thomas Jefferson, Thomas Paine, George Washington, Noah Webster. The list of notable names could be doubled, but these are, one hopes, enough to show that he brought to the convention not only an impressive aggregation of years but also an extraordinary range of experience.

Franklin's long life was a tale of four cities. He had known Puritan Boston, sober Philadelphia, imperial London, elegant Paris—and felt himself at home in all of them (Wright 1986, 11). In Boston he was repressed and then respected; in Philadelphia, accepted and then acclaimed; in official London, tolerated and then feared; in Paris, assessed and then adored.

STAYING IN HARNESS

Like many another man, Franklin approached old age with inconsistent goals. Even as early as 1765, at age fifty-eight, while still a colonial agent in London, Franklin said he sought "that retirement and repose with my little family, so suitable to my years" (Fleming 1972, 187). At this relatively early age the disposition to cease employment was probably mainly ceremonial. As the years continued to accumulate, however, Franklin expressed with increasing frequency and intensity his wish to escape the relentless pressures of public life. Yet the ingrained custom of being fully occupied was fostered by urgent requests for his continued services. Thus, pride reinforced habit, and Franklin again and again postponed and submerged his wish to leave the arena.

There is an additional factor that many old people will recognize in their own experience. Franklin *needed to be needed.* Such a drive seems especially powerful in people like Franklin whose early lives have been crowded with work and public responsibilities.

While still in Paris, the peace treaty having been signed, Franklin wrote ruefully, "It seems my Fate constantly to wish for Repose but never to obtain it" (Fleming 1972, 367). He had formally asked Congress to permit him to leave his post and return home. When, after a considerable delay, Congress made no response, Franklin asked a friend to press for an affirmative reply. Then, when Elias Boudinot, president of that same dilatory Congress, retired (at the ripe age of forty-three after serving eleven grueling months!) the septuagenarian Franklin sent Boudinot an effusive, ironical, Latin-laced, congratulatory letter. He could not, he wrote, "conceive a happier Being than the Man who, long laden with public Cares, and fatigued with every bodies Business, is allowed to enjoy *otium cum dignitate*" (Aldridge 1965, 325).

Once back home, and before the convention claimed him, Franklin found a balance, agreeable at least to himself, between public services and what he called "private amusements." For the latter he listed, in that order, conversation, books, his little garden, and cribbage. To offset such an unaccustomed load of idleness he found "public business enough to preserve me from ennui" (Van Doren 1938, 737).

The "public business" that barely protected Franklin from boredom was the highest office in Pennsylvania—president of the state council. As he explained to Bishop Shipley in England, "I was betrayed by some Remaining Ambition, from which I had imagined myself free . . . when the proper thing for me was Repose and a private Life" (Fleming, 390). He promised himself to serve only a single year, but he was persuaded to accept two reelections.

A month before the convention date, in a letter to Le Veillard, his former neighbor in Passy, Franklin reviewed his situation, "People who will drink the cup of life to the bottom must expect to meet with some of the usual dregs." But, he concluded equably, his stone was no worse. He would exercise with dumbbells, take hot baths, drink less wine, use bottled water imported from the springs of Passy (Clark 1983, 403), and profit from the medicinal values of blackberry jelly, one spoonful twice a day, to relieve pain (Aldridge 1965, 339).

THE FINAL FLING

During his last years in Paris, Franklin tried to extend his *Autobiography*. These efforts inevitably recalled the exploits and errors of his youth. He concluded, "Old Age is subject to Love and Follies as well as Youth." The amours of old age, while they last, seem ludicrous to the young; to the old they may be as serious but less addictive then before. In Franklin's case, his conduct in Paris society seems to have been marked mainly by provocative *billets-doux* and *bagatelles,* by daring talk, and by prudent (or at least cautious) conduct.

He had insistently (but unconvincingly) proposed marriage to Anne-Catherine Helvetius, that enchanting, independent, afflu- ent, neighborly widow who lived with a houseful of cats just down the road in Auteuil. Once back in Philadelphia, however, his most romantic letter to her reported that he hoped to be of further use to his country, adding chastely that they might meet again, not in this world but in the next.

There is no indication that Gallic "Follies" survived Franklin's return Atlantic crossing. Nor did new follies divert his attention from his duties as Pennsylvania's senior "Deputy" to the federal convention.

A PRESENT USEFULNESS

A very great difference in age separated Franklin from the other framers. He was twenty-six years older than Washington, forty-five years older than Madison, fifty-one years senior to Hamilton. He was old enough to have been the father of any of the delegates, and the grandfather of most of them.

One student has risked the guess that "A large majority of the Convention regarded the aged savant with the deference due to past performances rather than any regard for possible present usefulness. He had been long away from the young men, many of whom had worked together in frequent contact. They listened to his suggestions, then with little or no debate quietly voted the other way" (Lyon 1936, 73).

No doubt Franklin was respected, no doubt also that some of his ideas, like some proposed by other delegates, were ignored rather than considered. But when the convention reached a crisis, Frank- lin was quickly pressed into service. His election in July to the crucial Grand Committee on Compromise is a well-known exam- ple.

One should note also his role in September. The leading critics of the Constitution—Luther Martin, Lansing, Yates, Mercer—had gone home in anger. From the delegates remaining, at least three nonnegotiable negatives were expected. How many more might be enlisted to augment the opposition? How many last-minute recruits would it take to start a landslide that would bury the results of the convention? Suppose even one state delegation withheld its endorsement? In this crisis, Franklin was summoned by his younger colleagues to assure the necessary show of unity. This time, again, he provided a "present usefulness."

When it counted most, the delegates did not "quietly vote the other way." They called on Franklin.

PROPOSALS AND RESULTS

The accompanying table summarizes the twenty-seven[1] recorded proposals offered or supported by Franklin during the meeting. The outcomes may be organized in three groups:

Approved:	16 proposals
Rejected:	6 proposals
Not acted upon:	4 proposals

SIXTEEN PROPOSALS WERE APPROVED:
2. That state laws be consistent with treaties.
4. That the convention discuss the executive.
7. That the executive veto be limited.
9. That salary for House members be "fixed."
12. That a Committee on Representation be named.
13. That the committee report on representation be adopted.
14. That the committee report be considered as one "package."
15. That judges' salaries may be increased.
16. That the president be impeachable.
17. That the president be limited to one term.
18. That suffrage not be limited to freeholders.
19. That the naturalization policy be liberal.
20. That no property test for office-holders be required.
21. That "treason" be narrowly defined.
26. That no other emolument be paid the president.
27. That the signing of the Constitution be unanimous.

Proposals 2, 9, and 20 were approved by the convention without a roll-call vote, and (as Madison's *Notes* sometimes put it) *nemine contradicente,* or "without objection."

Proposals 13, 15, 16, 17, 18, 19, 21, and 26 were adopted by the roll-call votes shown in the table. These votes varied from a squeaker—the 5–4 compromise on representation in Congress—to solid such as the 8–3 tally on the definition of "treason"—to overwhelming such as the 7–1 vote against limiting the suffrage

Results of Franklin's Convention Proposals

No.	Date	Madison	Farrand	Proposal	Result
1	5/28	24	1:4	Temple Franklin for Secretary	Defeated, 2–5
2	5/31	44	1:4	Respect for treaties	Approved, nem. con.*
3	5/31	39	1:48	Unicameral legislature	Defeated, 1–6
4	6/1	45–8	1:65	Discuss the executive	6 speeches
5	6/2	51–5	1:626	No stipend for executive	Postponed
6	6/4	-	1:85; 102–3	Plural executive	Defeated, 0–10
7	6/4	65–6	1:94–8	Limit executive powers (Netherlands)	Compromise
8	6/5	67–8	1:119–20	Justices chosen by "Scottish" mode	Hoax
9	6/12	108	1:216; 427	"Fixed" pay for House members	Approved, nem. con.
10	6/26	198	1:219	No stipend for senators	Defeated, 5–6
11	6/28	209–10	1:450–2	Prayers in convention	No vote
12	6/30	226–7	1:485; 507	Seek compromise on representation	Approved
13	7/5	237–8	1:509	Committee reports Franklin's motion	Approved, 5–4
14	7/6	248	1:543	Compromise as "a package"	Approved
15	7/18	318	1:44	Permit increase in judge's salary	Approved, 6–2
16	7/20	332–34	1:65–67	President impeachable	Approved, 8–2
17	7/26	371	1:120	Limit president to one term	Approved, 7–3
18	8/7	401–5	1:236–49	Suffrage not limited to freeholders	Approved, 7–1
19	8/9	420–22	1:235	Liberal naturalization policy	Approved, 7–4
20	8/10	426–27	1:201–16	No property test for office	Approved, nem. con.
21	8/20	492	1:348	Narrow definition of treason	Approved, 8–3
22	9/7	601	1:542	Council of state	Defeated, 3–8
23	9/10	615	1:564	Proposed "second Convention"	Tabled
24	9/13	632	1:607	Committee on Economy	No report
25	9/14	638	1:615	Empower Congress to cut canals	Defeated, 2–8
26	9/15	645	1:628	No other emolument for president	Approved, 7–4
27	9/17	652–58	1:641–47	Unanimous signing	39 of 42 signed

*nem. con.: *nemine contradicente*, without objection
**later revised
"Date" refers to transaction in convention.
"Madison" and "Farrand" refer to the pages where the convention transaction is reported in Madison's *Notes* (1966) and Farrand's *Records* (1966).

to freeholders and the 8–2 vote that the president be impeachable.

Proposal 4 was not a formal motion. However, Franklin's suggestion that the issue of a single executive be discussed before a vote was taken brought an immediate response. That very day six declarations from five state delegations were offered.

Proposal 7 arose out of Franklin's vigorous and consistent opposition to a peremptory executive veto on legislation. He illustrated his position by the history both of the Netherlands and the British colonies in America. The present constitutional balance, involving a possible congressional override of a presidential veto, was developed in subsequent sessions of the Convention.

Proposal 12 led the convention at its next scheduled meeting to seek a compromise on the issue of congressional representation. Franklin urged each side to concede a little to accommodate contrasting opinions.

Proposal 14 deals with an important, perhaps crucial, tactical matter. The Committee on Compromise on July 5 made two recommendations *provided* that *both* recommendations be adopted by the convention. To avoid a situation in which representation in the Senate could be considered separately, Franklin said that he could only "vote for the whole together" (Madison 1966, 248).

Proposal 17, although approved by a 9–2 vote when a single seven-year term for the president was considered, was later revised. In its place a four-year term, with no explicit requirement on reelection, was approved. The example of George Washington set an effective, although not constitutionally required, limit of two terms until 1940.[2]

SIX PROPOSALS WERE DEFEATED:
1. That Temple Franklin be convention secretary
3. That the legislature be unicameral.
6. That the executive be plural.
10. That senators be unsalaried.
22. That a council of state be created.
25. That Congress be empowered to cut canals.

Results of these six roll-call votes are shown in the Table. Only one of them came close to adoption. Proposal 10, denying stipends for senators, lost 5–6.

Proposal 1 was not actually offered by Franklin. He was absent on the opening day when the nominations for convention secretary were made. No doubt Franklin backed it.

Proposal 3 has been included largely because of Madison's allusions to Franklin's preference for a single legislative chamber. Franklin himself did not, as a convention delegate, directly address the issue. Since Franklin actively favored a unicameral *state* legislature,[3] he would support it in principle at the national level.

Proposal 6 reflects a prevailing conclusion among Franklin's biographers that he wanted the convention to establish a plural executive. His convention speech about the executive was addressed to the issue of executive compensation. By inference it considers how many executives would be required. Before handing Wilson the text of his speech to read for him, Franklin offered an amendment that concludes "no salary, stipend, fee, or reward whatsoever for *their* services" (emphasis added). The speech contains other plurals—*men* of strong passions" who will "be your *rulers*." Later, after praising the unpaid services rendered by General Washington, Franklin asked, "Shall we doubt finding *three or four men* in all the United States with public spirit enough?" He answered his own question, "We shall never be without *a sufficient number* of wise and good *men* to undertake and execute well and faithfully the office in question."

The convention journal and the notes of delegate William Pierce also mention "The salaries of the *officers;* but *their* necessary expenses should be defrayed"[4] (Farrand 1966, 1:77–78, 91).

FOUR PROPOSALS WERE NOT ACTED ON:
  5. That no stipend be paid the executive
 11. That prayers be offered.
 23. That the Constitution be submitted to a second convention after review by Congress and state legislatures
 24. That a committee report on economy.

The nature of Proposals 5 and 11 is described elsewhere. Proposal 5 was seconded. Proposal 11 was seconded and discussed. Neither was put to a recorded vote.

Proposal 23, offered by Randolph during the final week of the convention and seconded by Franklin without other recorded comment, was tabled "for a day or two" and left on the table forever.

Proposal 24 did not originate with Franklin. It is included in the table because he was named on the committee and because its purpose was so fully consistent with his well-known opinions. Its terms of reference, "frugality, economy, and American manufactures," remain even today a hardy and probably indestructible perennial of national public concern and debate.

SUMMARY

If the four proposals that were not acted upon be set aside, twenty-two proposals offered or supported by Franklin remain.

Sixteen of these, or over 70 percent, were approved by the convention; the remaining six proposals, or just under 30 percent, were rejected.

CONCILIATION

Franklin's role as a convention delegate involved two types of activity: (1) seeking conciliation and compromise, and (2) advancing his own beliefs about basic requirements for good government.

We next consider his methods of arbitration and compromise. He has been described (Wright 1986, 12) as a man "made for conciliation and diplomacy." His devotion to compromise, however, was not complete. Cynical accommodations were unacceptable. Some bargains, like his boyhood purchase of a toy whistle, could cost too much. The best agreement was an improvement on either of the two alternatives.

Franklin's skills in conciliation were practised and sharpened during a lifetime of experience. He began to acquire the art in his early childhood. His father, Josiah Franklin, was often requested to arbitrate differences among contentious Boston neighbors, while around the family table, Josiah turned the attention of Benjamin and his other children "to what was good, just, and prudent in the Conduct of Life."

Franklin's own methods of resolving differences were varied. Four characteristics merit special notice. Briefly, they involved praise, the reputation of the intermediary, detachment, and diffidence.

PRAISE

The delegates in June had argued long, warmly, and inconclusively about many issues. Franklin began his major conciliatory speech by commending everyone for "great coolness and temper" during the preceding two weeks. "If anything of a contrary kind," he continued, "has on this occasion appeared, I hope it will not be repeated." Only then did he call on the delegates "to consult, not to contend."

He pointed out the dangers of fixed opinions and of a stubborn determination never to change them. He did not denounce these attitudes. He said only that such tactics were *ineffective*. "They neither enlighten nor convince us" (appendix A2).

"A spoonful of honey will catch more flies than a gallon of Vinegar," said Poor Richard. Franklin applied that proverb liberally. His dealings with Governor Randolph, leader of the crucial Virginia delegation, illustrate the principle.

Randolph had proposed that the executive "receive punctually at stated times a fixed compensation for the services rendered." Franklin felt obliged to differ. He did so very cautiously. As he began, he made it clear that his amendment affected only a small part of one of Randolph's fifteen proposed resolutions. He explained, too, how grateful he was to Randolph for the entire plan.

Later, the danger that Randolph might, for a variety of reasons, refuse to sign or support the Constitution, became a serious threat to the entire enterprise, for Virginia was the largest and most populous state. When, on 10 September, Randolph moved to refer the Constitution to a second Convention, Franklin seconded his motion. Clearly the proposal had no chance of passage. However, by seconding the motion Franklin did not affect the outcome and yet made it more difficult for Randolph to persist in dissent or to recruit supporters.

Still later, on the final day when Franklin offered his invitation to all delegates to join in unanimous support, Governor Randolph felt compelled to apologize for withholding his signature. He explained that he would not necessarily "oppose the Constitution without doors" and even assured the convention that "He meant only to be governed by his duty *as it should be prescribed by his future judgment*" (emphasis added).

Even then Franklin was not quite done with the softening process. He assured Randolph that he felt a high sense of obligation to him "for having brought forward the plan in the first instance and for the assistance he had given in its progress."

When in June 1788 the Constitution came before the Virginia state convention, Randolph actively supported ratification despite the eloquent indignation of Patrick Henry and the vituperation of George Mason. The vote was close. Randolph's support in Richmond, as contrasted with his opposition in Philadelphia, may well have been crucial. Ratification was approved 89–79 with two absentees. Thus a shift of only five votes (less than 3 percent of the total) would have kept Virginia out of the Union and Washington out of the presidency. That would have scuttled the ship of state before launching it. The Virginia vote was a delayed victory for Franklin's skill in dealing with Randolph.

In his famous speech of 17 September, Franklin impressively catalogued the handicaps to gaining agreement from the joint wisdom of a number of delegates. "You inevitably assemble with those men all their prejudices, their passions, their errors of opinion, their local interests, and their selfish views." But, he *carefully avoided* charging the delegates with these, or any other, frailties. They knew they possessed them, and he knew they knew. Still he managed to apply the catalogue to what *might* happen if some "other Convention" met to write a constitution. *This* convention, he assured them all, had "approached so near to perfection." The excellence of the product of *their* joint wisdom, he said, actually astonished him—"and I think it will astonish our enemies!"

Franklin almost invariably gave credit to those who differed with him for their efforts to advance the common good. People "generally like to be flattered," he once noted. "We are pleased with whatever suits our Pride" (Stourzh 1969, 8). "The honest man," he wrote, "will receive neither Money nor Praise that is not his due." True enough; but most men, honest or deceitful, exert their best efforts in response to praise. The acclaim should be clear enough to be audible, mild enough to be credible, and nicely proportioned to the situation, but (as Poor Richard saith):

> "A Flatterer never seems absurd;
> The Flatter'd always takes his word."

REPUTATION

The most effective conciliation requires more than adroitness. It requires also personal prestige and a record of success. The peacemaker succeeds in part because success is expected. Each achievement is enhanced by the previous success.

Franklin's skill as a conciliator was increasingly noted during the closing years of his life. Two years before the convention Franklin had returned from France to wild public acclaim for securing the French money and manpower essential for victory in the revolution. Franklin was, in those days, sometimes hailed as the "Father of his Country." This mark of public esteem was generally applied to Washington only after his unanimous election in 1789 as the nation's first president.

Franklin's reputation as philosopher and public servant made him a focus of attention in the months during and just preceding the convention. For example, General Horatio Gates, the grizzled veteran of Saratoga and Camden, watched with mounting chagrin the disintegration of the Union. He urged Franklin to become involved in national affairs. "No one but you," he concluded, "could hoop the barrel" (Aldridge 1965, 352). He saw Franklin not as one merely useful delegate from Pennsylvania but as the indispensable man to save the nation.

Back in Philadelphia, Franklin was endorsed for the Supreme Executive Council by both of the two major factions as well as by the organized mechanics of the city. In the election it became clear that he was expected to bridge the differences among them on state constitutional arrangements. These expectations were soon fulfilled. Franklin became, more than ever, a legend of success in his own time.

Benjamin Rush, the distinguished Philadelphia physician, patriot, and social reformer, observed with awe Franklin's conciliatory skills as applied in the state government. Franklin, he declared, "has destroyed party rage in our state or, to borrow an allusion from one of his discoveries, his presence and advice, like oil upon troubled waters, have composed the contending waves" (Warren, 58–59).

Meanwhile, *The Pennsylvania Packet* acclaimed the new hero as "the brightest luminary of the Western hemisphere." So Franklin's persuasive reputation exceeded the power of formal proof and generated conviction. The old philosopher incarnated the spirit of the Age of Enlightenment. Even John Adams, his severest critic, felt obliged to admit that Franklin's immense reputation was very nearly universal (Stourzh 1969, 3).

In short, the seventeen-year-old runaway apprentice who arrived in Philadelphia "fatigu'd and very hungry," with no possessions but a change of stockings and exactly one Dutch dollar, had become the most notable personality in his eighteenth-century world. Such a man, as amiable as he was eminent, could almost command conciliation even before proceeding to clarify differences and negotiate a middle ground.

DETACHMENT

A good negotiator gains effectiveness by a certain measure of aloofness. A conciliator may need to pose as indifferent even though he is not devoid of opinions of his own.

This asset, too, grew with age. As Franklin wrote to Madame Helvetius before leaving Paris, a man approaching eighty "looks out the window at the stir of those who pass by without taking part in their disputes" (Aldridge 1965, 266).

Such detachment can be powerfully assisted by a sense of personal rectitude. Franklin was a better negotiator because he could say and truly believe (whether it was invariably so or not) "that no human being could justly say, 'Ben Franklin has wronged me'" (Aldridge 1965, 362).

THE HUMBLE ENQUIRER

In the convention Franklin was dealing with experienced politicians, most of them distinguished lawyers, versed in the subtleties of bargaining, accustomed more to winning debates than to reconciling differences, not easily deceived by guile or slick talk. This environment severely tested his resources as a conciliator.

James Bryce, that shrewd English ambassador who taught Americans so much about their own government, once remarked that the Constitution was "the work of men who believed in original sin" (quoted in Kristol and Glazer 1987, 3). Franklin, like other framers, doubted the ability of mankind to govern itself without firm institutional constraints. Madison once wrote that if men were angels no government would be necessary. But he said that human conduct was often that of a *fallen* angel. Franklin expected human nature to be powerfully influenced by greed and push.

While young, Franklin tried with some success to develop a sophist's skills in debate. Having read of the rules of logic and the arts of rhetoric, he "put on the Humble Enquirer and Doubter." Thus he found he could embarrass and entangle opponents. After a few years he discarded most of these tricks but he did retain one—"the Habit of expressing myself in terms of modest Diffidence." He found this habit of considerable advantage, and his *Autobiography* quotes with relish from Pope's *Essay on Criticism:*

> Men must be taught as if you taught them not,
> And things unknown propos'd as things forgot.

Years later, continuing his *Autobiography* at Passy in 1784, Franklin noted the effect of his cultivated diffidence on his career. Humility, he wrote, was the last virtue added to his list. "I can not boast of much Success in acquiring the *Reality* of this Virtue, but I had a great deal with regard to the *Appearance* of it. . . . These Fifty Years past no one has heard a dogmatical Expression escape me." This trait, he believed, enabled him to exert great influence "in public Councils." For he thought he was a poor speaker, never eloquent, often at a loss for words, "yet I generally carried my

Point." Even if he could completely overcome his pride, he wryly admitted, "I should probably be proud of my Humility" (Lemay and Zoll 1986, 75–76).

TWO PRINCIPLES

Beyond the steady effort for conciliation and the dizzy multiplicity of detailed issues in Constitution-making, Franklin held fast to two basic requirements.

He desired, first, a simple orderly government that could operate effectively, without interruptions, and with a minimum of uncertainty.

Second, such a government, he believed, would have to engage the willing support and active participation of ordinary citizens.

PRAGMATISM

"Business ill-managed," said Franklin, "ruins faster than No Business." Government is a special kind of business; if well-administered it would be orderly, continuous, rational, snug, civil, and serene.

Like every other Convention delegate, Franklin had his personal doubts about some features of the completed draft Constitution. But, he thought it would *work.* It would replace the inefficient Articles of Confederation and might serve for an indefinite future. Another convention might produce a different constitution but it would not be likely to produce a better one. He therefore urged support for "*this* Constitution, because I expect no better and I am not sure it is not the best."

Furthermore, as a practical man who wanted his government to *work,* Franklin could support the Constitution because it contained a great self-adjusting mechanism. Article 5 provided two modes of amendment that, when ratified, "shall be valid to all Intents and Purposes, as Part of the Constitution. . . ." There is no record of Franklin's participation in the debates that led to Article 5, but the idea of the Constitution as a continuous experiment, with amendments developed by experience and new circumstances, was surely congenial to his scientific and pragmatic mind (Cohen 1985, 264).

In his salad days, Franklin had written a little book of metaphysical subtleties entitled "A Dissertation on Liberty and Necessity. . . ." The eighteen-year-old author regretted the booklet almost as soon as the ink dried on the 100 copies he printed. He burned most of the copies and included the entire episode among his many juvenile *errata*. In contrast, and much later, he perceived that his scientific experiments and their practical application helped bring him that international prestige so necessary to his diplomatic recognition and personal success. What, then, could be more natural than to extend the scientific approach to the task of government? Franklin did not first ask whether a public proposal was theoretically sound; rather, he asked first and last whether it would work (Rossiter 1953, 286).

In the convention, then, Franklin sought to apply the methods of orderly observation and close reasoning that had given rise to the new Society for Political Enquiries. With Franklin as its president, the society met regularly at his home. It was intended to remove the "complicated science of government" from the exclusive control of politicians and speculative theorists. Organized after the Annapolis Convention had proposed a Constitutional (or federal) Convention in Philadelphia and two weeks before the Continental Congress formally summoned the convention, the charter of the society provided useful clues to the expectations of Franklin and its other members in the year of the convention. "We have as yet," they declared, "accomplished but a partial independence." The revolution would be incomplete, they felt, until "a dependent people" freed themselves not only from the "fetters of foreign power" but also from the "influence of foreign prejudices" (from the charter, quoted in Connor, 106–7).

Dr. Benjamin Rush, Franklin's faithful friend and ardent admirer, and a member of the Society for Political Enquiries, summarizes the same viewpoint in a 1786 letter to a London friend. The American Revolution, he wrote, is not over. "We have only finished the first act of the great drama" (Historians 1987, 49).

For Franklin, reason (like every other human attribute) had its limits. As a means of evaluating human experience it is superb; as a means of curbing human nature it is at best inconclusive. Franklin admired the rational spirit but remained alert to its vulnerability. He was wryly aware, too, of the perils of self-deception in the use of reason. "So convenient a thing it is to be a *reasonable* Creature," he wrote in the *Autobiography*, "since it enables one to find or make a Reason for everything one has a mind to do" (Lemay and Zoll 1986, 28).

Madison and other convention delegates sometimes referred to the proposed Constitution as an "instrument." Franklin found that term congenial to his pragmatic point of view. He used it, for example, in his closing set speech when he urged every delegate to "put his name to this *instrument*." The word meant, in this context, a tool to accomplish a purpose, a means to an end. His regard for the Constitution as a way to get things done has reminded one commentator (Stourzh 1969, 13) of Gibbon's description of the public role of religion in Antonine Rome—"where all religions were considered equally false by the wise, equally true by the people, and equally useful by the magistrates."

Five months before he died, Franklin sent a short newsletter to Jean Baptiste Leroy, his former neighbor in France.

"Our new Constitution is now established," he reported, "and has an appearance that promises permanency; but in this world nothing can be said to be certain except death and taxes" (Fleming 1972, 403).

Most today recall only the last few ironic words of that quotation, especially while compiling an annual report to the Internal Revenue Service. Equally fundamental, however, is Franklin's belief that the Constitution *promised permanency*. Actually, the state ratifications had been recorded, the electors had met, the president had been installed, the Supreme Court established, and a Bill of Rights approved. All that in two years!

The Constitution was meeting, Franklin felt, the pragmatic test. His greatest single contribution to the convention was not a neat system of government but a powerful method of inquiry.

PARTICIPATION

The historian, Charles Beard, who tried diligently to identify the political and economic interests of each convention delegate, concluded that Franklin held "a more hopeful view of democracy than any other member of that famous group" (Beard 1935, 107). Indeed, before his efforts to reconcile differences and produce a workable plan of government, Franklin's chief aim was to enable ordinary citizens to take part in their government.

This concern was manifested in several ways, some of which were successful and some not. He urged a plural executive so that power would not be concentrated in a single person or group. In this he was unsuccessful.

English legal theory, as formulated by William Blackstone, the great eighteenth-century jurist, recognized three social orders: the Many, embodied in the House of Commons; the Few, in the House of Lords; and the One, in the person of the Monarch. Like other revolutionary leaders, Franklin did not want these distinctions in America. His break with that aspect of British political theory was sudden and complete. Loyal respect was replaced by a deadly hostility and rebellion.

Thomas Jefferson in 1776 drafted the first sentence of the Declaration of Independence to conclude that Americans "should declare the causes which impel them to threaten separation." Franklin, as a member of his small drafting committee, suggested that the word "threaten" be eliminated. Thus the text then (and now) reads "impel them to the separation." That small change in wording made the fracture irrevocable. Franklin was even more explicit in his letter to an English acquaintance: "You can have no treaty with us but as an independent state. Your Parliament never had a right to govern us, and your King has forfeited it by his bloody tyranny" (quoted in Eiselen 1928, 49–50).

Franklin spurned a suggestion that he accept an American peerage by royal decree (Eiselen 1928, chap. 12). He ridiculed the proposed hereditary qualifications for the Society of the Cincinnati. He first invented, and then gleefully destroyed, a proposal for hereditary professors of mathematics. He was active in the creation of a unicameral Pennsylvania state legislature, not only because it was simpler, more efficient, and cheaper, but also because it was not encumbered by an upper House to represent the Few of aristocracy, wealth, and privilege.

In his efforts on behalf of public participation in government, Franklin resisted proposals by other delegates (1) to limit the national suffrage to landholders, and (2) to require ownership of landed estates for eligibility to serve in Congress.

In July the Convention created a five-man Committee of Detail to prepare the crucial first draft on, among other matters, voting privileges in national elections. When the Convention considered the committee report on this question, Gouverneur Morris sought to limit the national suffrage to freeholders.[5] He was supported by several delegates, and opposed by others.

As the hour for adjournment neared, Franklin took the floor to oppose the amendment. He said that the suffrage was of great consequence to the common people. He did not think "that the elected" (i.e., the delegates at Philadelphia) "*had any right in any case,* to narrow the privileges of the electors," (i.e., the ordinary people at home).

When the vote came, as the convention adjourned for the day, Franklin's position prevailed, and Morris's motion was defeated, 7–1.

Picking its way, day by day and clause by clause, through the Committee of Detail report, the Convention on 10 August reached the proposal that the Congress, when later elected, should establish qualifications for its members "with regard to property."

Charles Pinckney of South Carolina promptly objected. The proposal, he said, meant that the first Congress would meet "without any particular qualifications of property." He assured his coleagues that he did not favor "an undue aristocratic influence." Still, holders of the important posts of legislator, executive, and judge should possess "competent property to make them independent and respectable." He was not ready to fix the exact value of such property, but surely the president should possess a "clear unencumbered estate" of at least $100,000; each judge and legislator should take an oath that his personal estate was worth at least $40,000.[6]

Pinckney was powerfully and promptly seconded by John Rutledge, also of South Carolina. As its delegation Chairman, he bluntly revealed why the Committee on Detail had been unable to agree on property qualifications, "being embarrassed by the danger of displeasing the people" if they set the qualifications too high and of frivolity if too low.

Franklin, again speaking extemporaneously, summarized the opposition to Pinckney's proposal. Franklin disliked "every thing that tended to debase the spirit of the common people." True, honesty and wealth could often be companions. True also, poverty was exposed to peculiar temptations. But some of the greatest rogues he knew were the richest rogues.

Pinckney's motion was "rejected by so general a *No*," that a roll call was not needed. After Franklin's speech the issue seemed settled, although, as sometimes happens in deliberative bodies, discussion continued.

Franklin's success on this point went further than the unanimous rejection of Pinckney's motion. The final text of the Constitution provides only that each house shall be the judge of its members' qualifications and that a representative must be at least twenty-five years old, hold citizenship for seven years, and live in the state he represents. Of freehold requirements, not a word.

One historian of the federal convention (Rossiter 1968, 213) has described Franklin's 10 August speech as one of his "finest moments." He met, head-on, a proposal to limit the access of ordinary people to positions of power—and won, convincingly.

FREE AND EASY

By August 1788 the convention was a year-old memory. The participating states had ratified the Constitution. Vigorous debates in the crucial states of New York and Virginia had produced votes uncomfortably close, but affirmative. The final months of Franklin's third year as president of the Pennsylvania Council were approaching. He let it be known at home and abroad that he would not be available for a fourth term. He had something else to do.

In these new circumstances Franklin resumed the often-promised and repeatedly deferred task of continuing to write his *Autobiography*. At Passy in 1784, awaiting his recall by Congress, Franklin had carried the leisurely account up to about 1728 and his "bold and arduous Project of arriving at moral Perfection." On the long voyage home, although urged by his friends to continue the memoir, he was distracted by what seemed at the time more opportune events. So he took the temperature of the Atlantic Ocean and wrote a treatise "On the Cause and Cure of Smoky Chimneys" (Van Doren 1938, 727–28).

But now, at long last, leisure and interest led him to resume the *Autobiography*. Many of Franklin's papers, which he expected to use as reminders, had been destroyed by British looters during the War, but he did find an interesting little paper of observations dated 9 May 1731. From this fifty-seven-year-old clue his narrative continued:

The great Affairs of the World . . . are carried on and effected by Parties.

The View of these Parties is their present general Interest, or what they take to be such.

The different Views of these different Parties occasion all Confusion.

While a Party is carrying on a general Design, each man has his particular private Interest in View.

Few in Public Affairs act from a mere View of the Good of their Country, whatever they may pretend. . . .

Fewer still in public Affairs act with a View to the Good of Mankind.

Reflecting in 1788 on these earlier observations about group behavior, Franklin must have noted how aptly they applied to his recent experience in preparing the new Constitution. He quoted them at length to start the last section of his life story. He recalled his youthful ambition to form "the Society of the Free and Easy" to be organized at the outset by "young and single Men only" and to be "kept a Secret."

Promotion of the society, he wrote, was postponed by the necessity of earning a living and then by "multifarious Occupations public and private." He still thought in 1788 "that it was a practicable Scheme, and might have been very useful." With a wistful revival of youthful assurance he wrote that "one Man of tolerable Abilities may work great Changes . . . among Mankind, if he first forms a good Plan and makes the Execution of that same Plan his sole Study and Business."

But now, really feeble at the last, he had to conclude, perhaps with a sigh, that he "no longer had Strength or Activity left sufficient for such an Enterprise."

CALENDAR MAY 25 to SEPTEMBER 17, 1787

SUN	MON	TUE	WED	THU	FRI	SAT
			MAY			
					25	26
27	28	29	30	31*		
			JUNE			
					1*	2*
3	4*	5*	6	7	8	9
10	11*	12*	13	14	15	16
17	18	19	20	21	22	23
24	25	26*	27	28*	29	30*
			JULY			
1	2	3	4	5	6*	7
8	9	10	11	12	13	14
15	16	17	18*	19	20*	21
22	23	24	25	26*	27	28
29	30	31				
			AUGUST			
			1	2	3	4
5	6	7*	8	9*	10*	11
12	13	14	15	16	17	18
19	20*	21	22	23	24	25
26	27	28	29	30	31	
			SEPTEMBER			
						1
2	3	4	5	6	7*	8
9	10*	11	12	13	14*	15*
16	17*					

No session on:
May 26, Rules Committee
June 14, drafting Federal Plan
July 3, Compromise Committee
July 4, Independence Day
July 27 to August 4,
    Committee of Detail
Sept. 11, Committee on
    Style
Sundays

* Days on which Franklin
spoke.

Appendices: Benjamin Franklin at the Constitutional Convention, Philadelphia, 1787

Appendix A
  Remarks Written by Franklin before Delivery
    A1. Ambition and Avarice (except two opening sentences), 2 June
    A2. To Consult, Not To Contend (except first sentence), 11 June
    A3. God Governs, 28 June
    A4. A Broad Table Is To Be Made (written in part), 30 June
    A5. Doubt a Little of his Own Infallibility, 17 September

Appendix B
  Remarks by Franklin Adapted from Madison's *Notes*
    B1. Executive Veto, 4 June
    B2. Executive Power: the Netherlands, 4 June
    B3. Choosing Judges; Scottish Procedure, 5 June
    B4. Salaries for Congress, 12 June
    B5. Control of Public Funds, 6 July
    B6. Impeaching the Executive, 20 July
    B7. Rulers as Servants, 26 July
    B8. Common People, 7 August
    B9. Friends Abroad, 9 August
    B10. The Greatest Rogues, 10 August
    B11. A Council of State, 7 September
    B12. A Rising Sun, 17 September

(Page numbers refer to the Ohio University Press Edition of Madison's *Notes*, 1966.)

Appendix C
  Note on Franklin's Use of a Sedan Chair at the Constitutional Convention

Appendix A: Remarks Written by Franklin before Delivery

APPENDIX A1.
AMBITION AND AVARICE
(2 JUNE; PP. 51–55)

With regard to compensation for the services of the Executive, I move to substitute "whose necessary expenses shall be defrayed, but who shall receive no salary, stipend, fee or reward whatsoever for their services."

Being very aware of the effect of age on my memory, I have been unwilling to trust to that for the observations which seem to support my motion, and have reduced them to writing that I might, with the permission of the Committee, read instead of speaking them.

[Wilson's offer to read Franklin's paper was accepted.]

Sir,

It is with reluctance that I rise to express a disapprobation of any one article of the plan for which we are so much obliged to the honorable gentleman [Mr. Randolph] who laid it before us. From its first reading I have borne a good will to it, and in general wished it success. In this particular of salaries to the Executive branch I happen to differ; and as my opinion may appear new and chimerical, it is only from a persuasion that it is right, and from a sense of duty that I hazard it. The Committee will judge of my reasons when they have heard them, and their judgment may possibly change mine. I think I see inconveniences in the appointment of salaries; I see none in refusing them, but on the contrary, great advantages.

Sir, there are two passions which have a powerful influence on the affairs of men. These are ambition and avarice; the love of power, and the love of money. Separately each of these has great force in prompting men to action; but when united in view of the same object, they have in many minds the most violent effects. Place before the eyes of such men, a post of *honour* that shall be at

151

the same time a place of *profit,* and they will move heaven and earth to obtain it. The vast number of such places it is that renders the British Government so tempestuous. The struggles for them are the true sources of all those factions which are perpetually dividing the Nation, distracting its Councils, hurrying sometimes into fruitless and mischievous wars, and often compelling a submission to dishonorable terms of peace.

And of what kind are the men that will strive for this profitable pre-eminence, through all the bustle of cabal, the heat of contention, the infinite mutual abuse of parties, tearing to pieces the best of characters? It will not be the wise and moderate, the lovers of peace and good order, the men fittest for the trust. It will be the bold and the violent, the men of strong passions and indefatigable activity in their selfish pursuits. These will thrust themselves into your Government and be your rulers. And these too will be mistaken in the expected happiness of their situation. For their vanquished competitors of the same spirit, and from the same motives will perpetually be endeavouring to distress their administration, thwart their measures, and render them odious to the people.

Besides these evils, Sir, though we may set out in the beginning with moderate salaries, we shall find that such will not be of long continuance. Reasons will never be wanting for proposed augmentations. And there will always be a party for giving more to the rulers, that the rulers may be able in return to give more to them. Hence as all history informs us, there has been in every State and Kingdom a constant kind of warfare between the governing and governed: the one striving to obtain more for its support, and the other to pay less. And this has alone occasioned great convulsions, actual civil war, ending either in dethroning of the Princes, or enslaving of the people. Generally indeed the ruling power carries its point, the revenues of princes constantly increasing, and we see that they are never satisfied, but always in want of more. The more the people are discontented with the oppression of taxes; the greater need the prince has of money to distribute among his partisans and pay the troops that are to suppress all resistance, and enable him to plunder at pleasure. There is scarce a king in a hundred who would not, if he could, follow the example of Pharaoh, get first all the people's money, then all their lands, and then make them and their children servants for ever. It will be said, that we don't propose to establish Kings. I know it. But there is a natural inclination in mankind to Kingly Government. It sometimes relieves them from Aristocratic domination. They had rather have one tyrant than five hundred. It gives more of the appearance of equality among Citizens, and that they like. I am apprehensive therefore, perhaps too apprehensive, that the Government of these States, may in future times, end in a Monarchy. But this catastrophe I think may be long delayed, if in our proposed system we do not sow the seeds of contention, faction and tumult, by making our posts of honor, places of profit. If we do, I fear that though we do employ at first a number, and not a single person, the number will in time be set aside. It will only nourish the fetus of a King, as the honorable gentleman from Virginia very aptly expressed it, and a King will the sooner be set over us.

It may be imagined by some that this is an Utopian idea, and that we can never find men to serve us in the Executive department, without paying them well for their services. I conceive this to be a mistake. Some existing facts present themselves to me which incline me to a contrary opinion. The High Sheriff of a County in England is an honorable office, but it is not a profitable one. It is rather expensive and therefore not sought for. But yet, it is executed and well executed, and usually by some of the principal Gentlemen of the County.

In France, the office of Counsellor or member of their Judiciary Parliaments is more honorable. It is therefore purchased at a high price: There are indeed fees on the law proceedings, which are divided among them, but these fees do not amount to more than three percent on the sum paid for the place. Therefore as legal interest is there at five percent they in fact pay two percent for being allowed to do the Judiciary business of the Nation, which is at the same time entirely exempt from the burden of paying them any salaries for their service. I do not however mean to recommed this as an eligible mode for our Judiciary department. I only bring the instance to show that the pleasure of doing good and serving their Country and the respect such conduct entitles them to, are sufficient motives with some minds to give up a great portion of their time to the public, without the mean inducement of pecuniary satisfaction.

Another instance is that of a respectable Society who have made the experiment, and practised it with success more than one hundred years. I mean the Quakers. It is an established rule with them, that they are not to go to law; but in their controversies they must apply to their monthly, quarterly and yearly meetings. Committees of these sit with patience to hear the parties, and spend much time in composing their differences. In doing this, they are supported by a sense of duty, and the respect paid to usefulness. It is honorable to be so employed, but it is never made profitable by salaries, fees, or perquisites. And indeed in all cases of public service the less the profit the greater the honor.

To bring the matter nearer home, have we not seen the great and most important of our offices, that of General of our Armies, executed for eight years together without the smallest salary, by a patriot whom I will not now offend by any other praise; and this through fatigues and distresses in common with the other brave men his military friends and companions, and the constant anxieties peculiar to his station? And shall we doubt finding three or four men in all the United States, with public spirit enough to bear sitting in peaceful Council for perhaps an equal term, merely to preside over our civil concerns, and see that our laws are duly executed? Sir, I have a better opinion of our Country. I think we shall never be without a sufficient number of wise and good men to undertake and execute well and faithfully the office in question.

Sir, the saving of the salaries that may at first be proposed is not an object with me. The subsequent mischiefs of proposing them are what I apprehend. And therefore it is, that I move the amendment. If it is not seconded or accepted I must be contented with the satisfaction of having delivered my opinion frankly and done my duty.

APPENDIX A2.
TO CONSULT, NOT TO CONTEND
(11 JUNE; PP. 99–103)

I have thrown my ideas of representation on a paper which Mr. Wilson will read to the Committee.

Mr. Chairman

It has given me great pleasure to observe that till this point, the proportion of representation, came before us, our debates were carried on with great coolness and temper. If any thing of a contrary kind, has on this occasion appeared, I hope it will not be repeated; for we are sent here to *consult,* not to *contend,* with each other; and declarations of a fixed opinion, and of determined resolution never to change it, neither enlighten nor convince us. Positiveness and warmth on one side, naturally beget their like on the other; and tend to create and augment discord and division in a great concern, wherein harmony and union are extremely necessary to give weight to our Councils, and render them effectual in promoting and securing the common good.

I must own that I was originally of opinion it would be better if every member of Congress, or our national Council, were to consider himself rather as a representative of the whole, than as an Agent for the interests of a particular State; in which case the proportion of members for each State would be of less consequence and it would not be very material whether they voted by States or individually. But as I find this is not to be expected, I now think the number of Representatives should bear some proportion to the number of the represented, and that the decisions should be by the majority of members, not by the majority of States. This is objected to from an apprehension that the greater States would then swallow up the smaller. I do not at present clearly see what advantage the greater States could propose to themselves by swallowing the smaller, and therefore do not apprehend they would attempt it.

I recollect that in the beginning of this Century when the Union was proposed of the two Kingdoms, England and Scotland, the Scotch patriots were full of fears, that unless they had an equal number of Representatives in Parliament, they would be ruined by the superiority of the English. They finally agreed however that the different proportions of importance in the Union of the two Nations should be attended to, whereby they were to have only forty members[1] in the House of Commons, and only sixteen in the House of Lords; a very great inferiority of numbers! And yet to this day I do not recollect that any thing has been done in the Parliament of Great Britain to the prejudice of Scotland; and whoever looks over the lists of public officers, civil and military, of that nation will find I believe that the North Britons enjoy at least their full proportion of emolument.

But, Sir, in the present mode of voting by States, it is equally in the power of the lesser States to swallow up the greater; and this is mathematically demonstrable. Suppose for example, that seven smaller States had each three members in the House, and the six larger have, one with another, six members; and that upon a question, two members of each smaller State should be in the affirmative and one in the Negative; they will make

Affirmatives .... 14 .... Negatives   7
And that all the larger States
     should be unanimously in
     the Negative, they would
     make .... Negatives   36
          In all.....................................   43

It is then apparent that the 14 carry the question against the 43, and the minority overpowers the majority, contrary to the common practice of assemblies in all countries and ages.

The greater States Sir are naturally as unwilling to have their property left in the disposition of the smaller, as the smaller are to have theirs in the disposition of the greater. An honorable gentleman has, to avoid this dificulty, hinted a proposition of equalizing the States. It appears to me an equitable one, and I should, for my own part, not be against such a measure, if it might be found practicable. Formerly, indeed, when almost every province had a different Constitution, some with greater others with fewer, privileges, it was of importance to the borderers when their boundaries were contested, whether by running the division lines, they were placed on one side or the other. At present when such differences are done away, it is less material. The interest of a State is made up of the interests of its individual members. If they are not injured, the State is not injured. Small States are more easily well and happily governed than large ones. If therefore in such an equal division, it should be found necessary to diminish Pennsylvania, I would not be averse to the giving a part of it to New Jersey, and another to Delaware. But as there would probably be considerable difficulties in adjusting such a division; and however equally made at first, it would be continually varying by the augmentation of inhabitants in some States, and their fixed proportion in others; and thence frequent occasion for new divisions, I beg leave to propose for the consideration of the Committee another mode, which appears to me to be as equitable, more easily carried into practice, and more permanent in its nature.

Let the weakest State say what proportion of money or force it is able and willing to furnish for the general purposes of the Union.

Let all the others oblige themselves to furnish each an equal proportion.

The whole of these joint supplies to be absolutely in the disposition of Congress.

The Congress in this case to be composed of an equal number of Delegates from each State.

And their decisions to be by the Majority of individual members voting.

If these joint and equal supplies should on particular occasions not be sufficient, let Congress make requisitions on the richer and more powerful States for farther aids, to be voluntarily afforded, leaving to each State the right of considering the necessity and utility of the aid desired, and of giving more or less as it should be found proper.

This mode is not new. It was formerly practised with success by the British Government with respect to Ireland and the Colonies. We sometimes gave even more than they expected, or thought just to accept; and in the last war carried on while we were united, they gave us back in five years a million Sterling. We would probably have continued such voluntary contributions, whenever the occasions appeared to require them for the common good of the Empire. It was not till they chose to force us, and to deprive us of the merit and pleasure of voluntary contributions that were refused and resisted. Those contributions however were to be disposed of at the pleasure of a Government in which we had no representative. I am therefore persuaded that they will not be refused to one in which the Representation shall be equal.

My learned Colleague [Mr. Wilson] has already mentioned that the present method of voting by States was submitted to originally by Congress, under a conviction of its impropriety, inequality, and injustice. This appears in the words of their Resolution. It is of Sept. 6, 1774. The words are

""Resolved that in determining questions in this Congress each Colony or province shall have one vote: the Congress not being possessed of, or at present able to procure, materials for ascertaining the importance of each Colony."

APPENDIX A3.
GOD GOVERNS
(28 JUNE; PP. 209–10)

Mr. President
The small progress we have made after four or five weeks close attendance and continual reasonings with each other, our different sentiments on almost every question, several of the last producing as many noes as ayes, is methinks a melancholy proof of the imperfection of the human understanding. We indeed seem to feel our own want of political wisdom, since we have been running about in search of it. We have gone back to ancient history for models of Government, and examined the different forms of those Republics which having been formed with the seeds of their own dissolution, now no longer exist. And we have viewed Modern States all round Europe, but find none of their Constitutions suitable to our circumstances.

In this situation of this Assembly, groping as it were in the dark to find political truth, and scarce able to distinguish it when presented to us, how has it happened, Sir, that we have not hitherto once thought of humbly applying to the Father of Lights to illuminate our understandings? In the beginning of the contest with Great Britain, when we were sensible of danger, we had daily prayer in this room for the divine protection. Our prayers, Sir, were heard, and they were graciously answered. All of us who were engaged in the struggle must have observed frequent instances of a superintending Providence in our favor. To that kind Providence we owe this happy opportunity of consulting in peace on the means of establishing our future national felicity. And have we now forgotten that powerful Friend? Or do we imagine that we no longer need His assistance? I have lived, Sir, a long time, and the longer I live, the more convincing proofs I see of this truth— *that God Governs in the affairs of men.* And if a sparrow cannot fall to the ground without His notice, is it probable that an empire can rise without His aid? We have been assured, Sir, in the sacred writings, that "except the Lord build the house they labour in vain that build it." I firmly believe this; and I also believe that without His concurring aid we shall succeed in this political building no better than the Builders of Babel. We shall be divided by our little partial local interests; our projects will be confounded, and we ourselves shall become a reproach and by-word down to future ages. And what is worse, mankind may hereafter from this unfortunate instance, despair of establishing Governments by Human wisdom and leave it to chance, war and conquest.

I therefore beg leave to move that henceforth prayers imploring the assistance of Heaven, and its blessings on our deliberations be held in this Assembly every morning before we proceed to business, and that one or more of the Clergy of this City be requested to officiate in that Service.

APPENDIX A4.
A BROAD TABLE IS TO BE MADE
(30 JUNE; PP. 226–27)

The diversity of opinions turns on two points. If a proportional representation takes place, the small States contend that their liberties will be in danger. If an equality of votes is to be put in its place, the large States say their money will be in danger. When a broad table is to be made, and the edges of planks do not fit, the artisan takes a little from both, and makes a good joint. In like manner here both sides must part with some of their demands, in order that they may join in some accommodating proposition.

I have prepared a proposition which I shall read. It may lie on the table for consideration.

"That the Legislatures of the several States shall choose and send an equal number of Delegates, namely—who are to compose the second branch of the General Legislature.

"That in all cases or questions wherein the Sovereignty of individual States may be affected, or whereby their authority over their own Citizens may be diminished, or the authority of the General Government within the several States augmented, each State shall have equal suffrage.

"That in the appointment of all Civil officers of the General Government in the election of whom the Second branch may by the Constitution have part, each State shall have equal suffrage.

"That in fixing the Salaries of such officers, and in all allowances for public services, and generally in all appropriations and dispositions of money to be drawn out of the General Treasury; and in all laws for supplying that Treasury, the Delegates of the several States shall have suffrage in proportion to the sums which their respective States do actually contribute to the Treasury."

Where a ship had many owners this was the rule of deciding on her expedition. I was one of the Ministers from this Country to France during the joint war. I would have been very glad if allowed a vote in distributing the money to carry it on.

APPENDIX A5.
DOUBT A LITTLE OF HIS OWN INFALLIBILITY
(17 SEPTEMBER; PP. 653–54)

The engrossed Constitution being read, Dr. Franklin rose with a speech in his hand, which . . . Mr. Wilson read in the words following:

Mr. President

I confess that there are several parts of this constitution which I do not at present approve, but I am not sure I shall never approve them. For having lived long, I have experienced many instances of being obliged by better information, or fuller consideration, to change opinions even on important subjects, which I once thought right, but found to be otherwise. It is therefore that the older I grow, the more apt I am to doubt my own judgment, and to pay more respect to the judgment of others. Most men indeed, as well as most sects in Religion, think themselves in possession of all truth, and that wherever others differ from them it is so far error. Steele, a Protestant, in a dedication tells the Pope, that the only difference between our Churches in their opinions of the certainty of their doctrines is, the Church of Rome is infallible and the Church of England is never in the wrong. But though many private persons think almost as highly of their own infallibility as of that of their sect, few express it so naturally as a certain French lady, who in a dispute with her sister, said "I don't know how it happens, Sister, but I meet with nobody but myself that's always in the right—*Il n'y a que moi qui a toujours raison.*"

In these sentiments, Sir, I agree to this Constitution with all its faults, if they are such; because I think a general Government necessary for us, and there is no form of government but what may be a blessing to the people if well administered, and believe farther that this is likely to be well administered for a course of years, and can only end in Despotism, as other forms have done before it, when the people shall become so corrupted as to need Despotic Government, being incapable of any other. I doubt too whether any other Convention we can obtain, may be able to make a better Constitution. For when you assemble a number of men to have the advantage of their joint wisdom, you inevitably assemble with those men, all their prejudices, their passions, their errors of opinion, their local interests, and their selfish views. From such an assembly can a perfect production be expected? It therefore astonishes me, Sir, to find this system approaching so near to perfection as it does; and I think it will astonish our enemies, who are waiting with confidence to hear that our councils are confounded like those of the Builders of Babel; and that our States are on the point of separation, only to meet hereafter for the purpose of cutting one another's throats. Thus I consent, Sir, to this Constitution because I expect no better, and because I am not sure that it is not the best. The opinions I have had of its errors, I sacrifice to the public good. I have never whispered a syllable of them abroad. Within these walls they were born, and here they shall die. If every one of us in returning to our Constitents were to report the objections he has had to it, and endeavor to gain partisans in support of them, we might prevent its being generally received, and thereby lose all the salutary effects and great advantages resulting naturally in our favor among foreign Nations as well among ourselves, from our real or apparent unanimity. Much of the strength and efficiency of any Government, in procuring and securing happiness to the people, depends on opinion, on the general opinion of the goodness of the Government, as well as of the wisdom and integrity of its Governors. I hope therefore that for our own sakes as a part of the people, and for the sake of posterity, we shall act heartily and unanimously in recommending this Constitution (if approved by Congress and confirmed by the Conventions) wherever our influence may extend, and turn our future thoughts and endeavors to the means of having it well administered.

On the whole, Sir, I can not help expressing a wish that every member of the Convention who may still have objections to it, would with me, on this occasion doubt a little of his own infallibility, and to make manifest our unanimity, put his name to this instrument.

I move that the Constitution be signed by the members in the following convenient form: "Done in Convention by the unanimous consent of *the States* present the Seventeenth Day of September in the Year of our Lord One Thousand Seven Hundred and Eighty-seven and of the Independence of the United States of America the Twelfth; In Witness wherof we have hereunto subscribed our names."

Appendix B: Remarks by Franklin Adapted from Madison's *Notes*

APPENDIX B1.
EXECUTIVE VETO
(4 JUNE; P. 62)

I am sorry to differ from my colleague [Mr. Wilson], for whom I have a very great respect, on any occasion, but I can not help it on this matter of giving the Executive an absolute veto on the laws.

I had some experience of this check, by the Executive on the Legislature, under the proprietary government of Pennsylvania. The veto of the Governor was then constantly used to extort money. No good law whatever could be passed without a private bargain with him. An increase of his salary, or some donation, was always made a condition. At last it became the regular practice to have Treasury orders in his favor presented along with the bills to be signed, so that he might actually receive the former before he signed the latter.

When the Indians were scalping the Western people, and news of it arrived, the concurrence of the Governor in the means of self-defense could *not* be got until it was agreed that his Estate should be exempted from taxation. So the people were to fight for the security of his property, whilst he bore no share of the burden. This was a mischievous sort of check!

If the Executive had a Council, such a power would be less objectionable. As has been said, the King of Great Britain has not exerted his veto since the Revolution. But that is easily explained. Bribes and emoluments now given to the members of Parliament render the veto unnecessary, everything being done according to the will of the Ministers.

I fear that, if a veto is given as proposed, more power and money will be demanded until at last enough would be got to influence and bribe the Legislature into a complete subjection to the will of the Executive.

APPENDIX B2
EXECUTIVE POWER: THE NETHERLANDS
(4 JUNE; PP. 65–66)

A Gentleman from South Carolina [Pierce Butler] a day or two ago called our attention to the case of the United Netherlands. I wish he had been a little more complete and had gone back to the origin of that Government. The people, being under great obligations to the Prince of Orange, whose wisdom and bravery had saved them, chose him for Stadtholder [Chief of State]. He did very well. Inconveniences however were felt from his powers which, growing more and more oppressive, were at length set aside. Still there was a party for the Prince of Orange which was inherited by his son who excited insurrections, spilled a great deal of blood, murdered the de Witts, and got the old powers returned to the Stadtholder. Afterwards another Prince had power to excite insurrections and to make the Stadtholdership hereditary. The present Stadtholder is willing to wade through a bloody Civil War to establish a monarchy.

Colonel Mason has mentioned the danger in appointing officers. I know how that would be managed. As it used to be in Pennsylvania, no new appointment would be tolerated unless it be referred to the Executive. Thus, all profitable offices will be at his disposal. The first man put at the helm will be a good one. Nobody knows what sort may come afterwards. The Executive will always be increasing, here as elsewhere, until it ends in a Monarchy.

APPENDIX B3
CHOOSING JUDGES: SCOTTISH PROCEDURE
(5 JUNE; PP. 67–68)

Two modes of choosing Judges have been mentioned; to wit, by the Legislature and by the Executive. I wish such other modes to be suggested as may occur to other gentlemen; it is a point of great moment. I will mention one which, I understand, was practiced in Scotland. In the Scotch mode the nomination proceeds from the Lawyers, who always select the ablest of the profession in order to get rid of him, and share his practice among themselves. Here, too, it should always be in the interest of the electors to make the best possible choice.

APPENDIX B4
SALARIES FOR CONGRESS
(12 JUNE; P. 108)

I approve the amendment to render the salaries of Congress as fixed as possible, but I dislike the word "liberal." I prefer "moderate" if it is necessary to substitute any other. The tendency of abuses, in every case, is to grow of themselves when once begun. Consider the progress of ecclesiastical benefices from the unpaid service of the Apostles to the establishment of the Papal system.

(26 June; P. 198)

I second General Pinckney's motion to allow no salary to Senators. I wish the Convention to stand fair with the people. There are in it a number of young men who will probably be Senators. If lucrative appointments are recommended we may be charged with having carved out places for ourselves.

APPENDIX B5
CONTROL OF PUBLIC FUNDS
(6 JULY; PP. 251–52)

I do not mean to go into a justification of the Report of the Committee on Compromise, but as it has been asked what is the use of restraining the Second Branch from meddling with money bills, I must say that it is always important that the people know who spent their money, and how it is spent. It is a maxim that those who feel can best judge. This end will, I think, be best attained if money affairs are confined to the immediate representatives of the people. This was my inducement to concur in the report.

As to the danger and difficulty that might arise from a veto in the Second Branch where the people are not proportionally represented, it may easily be avoided by declaring that there shall be no such veto. Or, if that will not do, by declaring that there shall be no such Second Branch at all.

APPENDIX B5
IMPEACHING THE EXECUTIVE
(20 JULY; PP. 332, 334)

I am for retaining the provision for the removal of the Executive on impeachment and conviction for malpractice or neglect of duty. This clause is favorable to the Executive. History furnishes one example only of a first Magistrate being formally brought to public Justice. Everybody cried out against this as unconstitutional!

What was the practice before this in cases where the chief Magistrate rendered himself obnoxious? Why, recourse was to assassination in which he was deprived not only of his life but also of the opportunity of vindicating his character. It is the best way therefore to provide in the Constitution for the regular punishment of the Executive when his misconduct deserves it and for his honorable acquital when he is unjustly accused. . . .

Consider the case of the Prince of Orange during the late war. Under an agreement between France and Holland, their two fleets were to unite at a certain time and place. The Dutch fleet did not appear. Everybody began to wonder about it. At length it was suspected that the Prince was at the root of the matter. This suspicion grew. Yet, as the Prince could not be impeached and no regular inquiry took place, he remained in office, strengthening his own party. As the party opposed to him became formidable, his behavior gave rise to the most violent animosities and contentions. Had the Prince been impeachable, a regular and peaceable inquiry would have taken place. He would, if guilty, have been duly punished; if innocent, restored to the confidence of the public.

APPENDIX B7
RULERS AS SERVANTS
(26 JULY; P. 371)

In considering the term of office for the Executive some seem to imagine that the Magistrate would be degraded by returning him to the mass of the people. I hold this view to be contrary to republican principles. In free Governments, the rulers are the servants, and the people are their superiors, and sovereigns. Therefore to return the rulers among the people is not to *degrade* them but to *promote* them. It would be imposing an unreasonable burden on the rulers to keep them always in a state of Servitude, and not allow them to become again one of the Masters.

APPENDIX B8
COMMON PEOPLE
(7 AUGUST; P. 404)

It is of great consequence that we not undervalue the virtue and public spirit of our common people, of which they displayed a great deal during the war, and which contributed most to its favorable outcome. I recall the honorable refusal of the American seamen, who were taken in great numbers to British Prisons during the war, to redeem themselves from misery or to seek their fortunes by serving aboard the Ships of the Enemies of their own Country. Contrast their patriotism with a contemporary instance of British seamen who, made prisoners by the Americans, readily boarded our ships on being promised a share of the prizes that might be made out of their own country. The difference, I believe, proceeded from the different manner in which the common people were treated in America and in Great Britain. I do not think, in any case, that the elected have any right to narrow the privileges of the electors.

The British Statute, setting forth the danger of tumultuous meetings and, on that pretext, narrowing the suffrage to persons having freehold property of a certain value, is arbitrary. I notice that this Statute was soon followed by another, enacted by the succeeding Parliament, subjecting people who had no votes to peculiar labors and hardships.

I am persuaded also that such a restriction as is proposed here would create great uneasiness in the populous States. The sons of a substantial farmer, not being themselves freeholders, would not be pleased to be disfranchised,—and there are a great many such persons.

APPENDIX B9
FRIENDS ABROAD
(9 AUGUST; P. 422)

I am not against fixing a reasonable time for new citizens to become eligible to serve in the Senate. But I would be very sorry to see anything illiberal in the Constitution. The people in Europe are friendly to this Country. Even in Great Britain we have now, and had even during the recent war, many friends, not only among the people at large but also in both houses of Parliament. In every other Country in Europe all the people are our friends.

In the course of the Revolution we found that many strangers served us faithfully,—even while many native Americans took part against their Country. When foreigners, after searching for some other Country in which they can obtain more happiness, give preference to ours, it proves an attachment which ought to excite our confidence and affection. . . .

I remind the Convention that an omission of a restriction in the Constitution does not mean that all the persons in question would actually be chosen members of the Legislature.

APPENDIX B10
THE GREATEST ROGUES
(10 AUGUST; PP. 426–27)

I dislike everything that tends to debase the spirit of the common people. If honesty is often the companion of wealth, and if poverty is exposed to peculiar temptation, it is not less true that the possession of property increases the desire for more property.

Some of the greatest rogues I ever knew were the richest rogues. Let us remember the character that the Scripture requires in Rulers: they should be men hating covetousness.

This Constitution will be much read and noticed in Europe. If it betrays a great partiality to the rich, it will not only hurt us in the esteem of the most liberal and enlightened men there, but also discourage common people from migrating to this Country.

APPENDIX B11
A COUNCIL OF STATE
(7 SEPTEMBER; P. 601)

I second the motion by Colonel Mason to instruct the Committee to prepare a clause or clauses to establish an Executive Council, as a Council of State, for the President of the United States, to consist of six members, two from the Eastern, two from the Middle, and two from the Southern States, with a rotation and duration of office similar to those for the Senate, such Council to be appointed by the Legislature or by the Senate.

We seem to fear too much cabals in appointments by a group, and to have too much confidence in appointments by one person. Experience shows that caprice, the intrigues of favorites and mistresses, etc., are most prevalent in monarchies. Among instances of abuse in such modes of appointment, consider the many bad Governors appointed in Great Britain for the Colonies. In my opinion a Council would not only be a check on a bad President but also be a relief to a good one.

APPENDIX B12
A RISING SUN
(17 SEPTEMBER; P. 659)

(While the delegates were signing their names, Dr. Franklin— looking towards President Washington's chair, on the back of which a sun was painted—said to a few members nearby:)

Painters have found it difficult to distinguish in their art a rising from a setting sun. I have often and often in the course of the Session, and the vicissitudes of my hopes and fears as to its issue, looked at the sun at the back of the President without being able to tell whether it is rising or setting. But now at length I have the happiness to know that it is a rising and not a setting sun.

Appendix C: Note on Franklin's Use of a Sedan Chair at the Constitutional Convention

Franklin's uncertain health during the Constitutional Convention is mentioned by all biographers. The regular use of a sedan chair is often cited as evidence of Franklin's frailty.

The Historical Society of Pennsylvania wrote me in March 1985 that a sedan chair is displayed in the State House with the following Plaque:

> By the close of his diplomatic career in Paris Dr. Franklin's health had deteriorated and he had difficulty walking. He brought back from Europe with him the first sedan chair to be seen in Philadelphia and was carried upon it to the Pennsylvania State House during his attendance at the Constitutional Convention in 1787. This is similar to the one he used.

The Society is unable to provide any further information about the reported use of a sedan chair.

More details on the topic are supplied in *Miracle at Philadelphia* by Catherine Drinker Bowen than in any other book. She writes:

> On Monday [the second Convention session] Dr. Franklin . . . came to the State House in a sedan chair which he had brought from Paris. . . . Four husky prisoners from the Walnut Street jail bore the cheerful cargo. . . . Up five steps to the State House went the little procession and into the East room where the bearers set down their burden beside the Bar (34–35).

and

> [On the final Convention day] Franklin's sedan chair lumbering into view, the prisoners carrying their stout burden up the State House steps. Already the scene took on the quality of nostalgia, as of something customary. . . . (254).

Mrs. Bowen's bibliography gives no sources for the above picturesque details, but she refers readers to the notes she kept. These notes, now in the Manuscript Division, Library of Congress, include a long editorial memorandum that asks many questions about her manuscript. One of these questions asks where Mrs. Bowen obtained detailed information about the sedan chair. She replied by writing across this section of the editor's memorandum: "Nat. Indep. Hist. Park."

Upon application to the National Independence Historical Park, I was sent a copy of page 122, Part D, from the Suggestions for Equipping the Assembly Room. The full text of this material, including Footnote 166, follows:

Franklin's Sedan Chair

In order to attend the sessions of the Constitutional Convention of 1787 with some degree of comfort, Franklin was carried from Franklin Court to the bar of the Assembly Room in a sedan chair[166] he had presumably recently brought from France. As this was perhaps the first conveyance of its kind seen in Philadelphia, it was probably 'parked' outside the bar in a corner to keep it away from the public, in the State House central hall.

It is suggested that an eighteenth century, plain, leather covered, sedan chair be acquired and placed in a corner of the Assembly Room gallery area, as an indication of the attendance of Franklin at the Constitutional Convention.

---

166. ". . . a Sedan-chair, in which I have often seen him carried by two men, to and from the State House, when he was President of the Supreme Executive Council of Pennsylvania. This Sedan-chair was sent to the Pennsylvania Hospital, where it remained a great many years, in the garret; but on inquiry about it, lately, I ascertained that it had been broken up and burned." Col. Robert Carr, "Personal Recollections of Benjamin Franklin,"*The Historical Magazine*, IV, second series (Aug. 1868), pp. 59, 60.

Franklin lived in Philadelphia from 14 September 1785 to his death on 17 April 1790—fifty-five months. I can find no evidence that the chair was used by him, either regularly or occasionally, during the four months the Constitutional Convention was meeting. Nor have I been able to find evidence that it was carried by "four husky prisoners from the Walnut Street jail."

Colonel Robert Carr remembered only two men and did not mention where or how they were recruited. In any case, Franklin, according to Col. Carr's memory, could have used his sedan chair at any time during the three years he was President of the Supreme Executive Council of Pennsylvania.

Fleming (1971, 482) says clearly that Franklin, after his return to Philadelphia, "*trudged* almost daily" between his home and the State House. This means that Franklin often climbed up and down steps in addition to his walks along the street. He climbed stairs every day in his home to reach his library and his bedroom on the second floor. The door-to-door distance from his house on Franklin Place to Independence Hall is barely three hundred yards, on level ground.

Clark, in his account of the convention, does not mention the use of the sedan chair in that connection. Clark does say that a year *after* the Convention (August 1788) Franklin was taking opium to deaden the pain of the stone, that he could scarcely move, and was "carried in a sedan chair by two men from the local prison" (1983, 412). Other more recent writers (Collier 1986, 78) say that for two weeks *before* the Convention Franklin went daily to the State House in a Sedan Chair "carried by prison trusties." No source is given nor is it said the chair was used during the convention. The explicit statment that Franklin during the convention was "too weak to walk" (Burress 1987, 5) is supported by no other writer or by the records of contemporary observers. It is remarkable how Madison's observation that it was "inconvenient to the doctor to remain long on his feet" (Madison 1966, 18) has been, over the decades, extrapolated to render Franklin completely incapacitated. Meanwhile, too, the knowledge of how the sedan was moved has increased so that it can now be reported that it was borne by four acrobatic prisoners who "with lumbering strides" somehow balanced the sedan poles *on their shoulders* (Mc-Caughey 1987, 21).

There is, finally, a first-hand, contemporary record that strongly suggests that Franklin rarely, if ever, found it necessary to use a sedan chair at the Constitutional Convention. Writing to his sister, Mrs. Jane Mecom, just three days after the Convention adjourned, Franklin said that he had "attended the Business of it 5 Hours in every Day from the beginning; which is something more than four Months. You may judge from thence that my health continues; some tell me I look better, and they suppose the *daily* Exercise of *going and returning* from the State-house has done me good" (emphasis added) (Farrand 1966, 20 September, 3:98).

Several letters to the Historian of the Independence National Historical Park, sent in December 1984 and April 1985 have elicited no further reply or information.

In summary, references to the sedan chair as evidence of Franklin's frailty and limited effectiveness as a convention delegate should be regarded with great caution.[1]

Notes

CHAPTER 1. EVALUATIONS

1. In 1787 two states—Georgia and Pennsylvania—had unicameral legislatures. They became bicameral in 1789 and 1790, respectively. Only one state today (Nebraska, since 1934) had a unicameral legislature.

CHAPTER 2. PLACES AND PEOPLE

1. Polly was the daughter of Franklin's London landlady in Craven Street. She was attracted by Franklin's account of the social graces of Philadelphia, lived there while the convention was meeting, and read to Franklin during his illness in 1788 (Clark 1983, 415).

CHAPTER 3. VEXATIOUS DELAYS

1. Bassett, Blair, Brearley, Broom, Butler, Fitzsimmons, King, Madison, R. Morris, C. Pinckney, C. C. Pinckney, Read, Rutledge, Spaight, Washington, Williamson, Wilson. Several of these delegates were absent for weeks in the interval between opening and closing sessions.
2. John Brown Cutting, briefly enrolled at the Inner Temple in London, was a friend and correspondent of Adams and Jefferson.
3. The state resolutions naming Maryland delegates were dated 26 May 1787. The assembly had in fact voted to pay its convention delegates like its delegates to the Continental Congress (Farrand 1966, 3:586).

CHAPTER 4. THE PEOPLE WILL NEVER . . .

1. This proclamation that any dire fate was better than accepting a decision by the convention was reiterated by other delegates. John Dickinson, for instance, declared "we would sooner submit to a foreign power than . . . be thrown under the domination of the large states." Dickinson had spent most of his adult life in Pennsylvania, and had served in its assembly, but he was at the moment a delegate of Delaware and spoke accordingly (Madison 1966, 118; Burress 1987, 7).

CHAPTER 5. WORDS, WORDS . . .

1. McHenry had been impressed by Franklin's speech of 17 September, calling it "plain, insinuating, and persuasive" (Peters 1987, 212). His later

explanation of his own reasons for signing the Constitution echoes, almost word for word, the arguments advanced by Franklin. McHenry, however, added two other forceful points on his own: (1) that Amendments could remedy any errors the Constitution might contain; and (2) that the outlook under the Articles of Confederation was completely hopeless (Warren 1967, 717).

CHAPTER 6. CONTROVERSY

1. Mansfield resigned the next year, 1788. Wilson's reference to him was not irrelevant to American memories. In London in 1760 Franklin and Lord Mansfield reached a compromise on the tax liability of the Penn family. Later, Mansfield ruefully acknowledged the effectiveness of Franklin's satires on British colonial policy. Mansfield was also known to some American statesmen by his ruling in favor of James Somersett, a slave brought to England in 1772: that English law did not permit an owner to transport a slave out of the country (quoted in Seldes 1968, 317). The decision was interpreted to mean that the English air was to pure for slavery, or (in Blackstone's earlier dictum) a slave in England, protected by English law, "with regard to all natural rights becomes *eo instanti* a free man" (Taylor 1937, 83). Men concerned with fugitive slave legislation must have been interested in this decision. *The Task*, Cowper's widely read poem published in 1785, refers to Mansfield's ruling: "Slaves can not breathe in England; if their lungs / Receive our air, that moment they are free."

2. These two words echo Franklin's 2 June convention address. The alliterative phrase pairing ambition and avarice was common in the eighteenth century. Franklin paired the two as "social passions" as early as 1728 (Stourzh 1969, 15).

3. The General and his new young wife had travelled from Charleston to Philadelphia by boat and both had been seasick in rough weather (Burns 1982, 30–42).

4. A description of events in the Philadelphia convention can scarcely be stretched to include action in another forum by a different body. Yet passing reference at least should be made to the adoption in New York on 13 July 1787 of the Northwest Ordinance. In Article VI the Continental Congress forbade the introduction of slavery in all that vast area.

The sponsor of Article VI did not expect it to be adopted. Introduced at the last minute, it was not in the preliminary draft of 11 July. The presiding officer was a Virginian. Most of the eighteen delegates present were little known; the "powerful" delegates were busy in Philadelphia. In 1789 the first United States Congress re-enacted the ordinance with little protest (Davis, 75–76; Berthoff, 37).

Volumes have been published to explain the contrast between the debates in Philadelphia on every slavery-related issue and the serene agreement in New York. This is not the place to add to that impressive bibliography. We may leave it by remarking that it is always easier to write on a clean page.

CHAPTER 10. CHRONOLOGY: COMPROMISE ON REPRESENTATION

1. Funeral oration by Mirabeau, seconded by Lafayette and La Rochefoucauld.

2. Williamson, generally listed as merchant and physician, was also a qualified clergyman (Mitchell and Mitchell 1964, 64). Although not "of the clergy of this City" (as suggested by Franklin's motion), Williamson could have prayed for the Convention without pay and, under the secrecy rule, only God would have known about it. Delegate Abraham Baldwin of Georgia had also been consecrated to the clergy after training at Yale and had been for five years a chaplain in the Continental Army. He did not volunteer to pray for nothing, either.

3. Coxe was also an active member of the Society for Political Enquiries and had been a delegate, the previous year, to the Annapolis Convention.

4. New Hampshire delegates had not yet arrived; New York's delegation had left for home.

CHAPTER 11. CHRONOLOGY: OTHER ISSUES

1. The State of Franklin existed 1784–88. It had an elected governor, other officials, a senate, a house, and organized armed forces. It issued its own currency; and applied to the Continental Congress for recognition as a state. Correspondence on this application with various leaders, including Benjamin Franklin, continued through 1787. Franklin was informed in 1786 that the people of the region had named their state after him "as a testimony of the high esteem they have. . . ." He acknowledged the honor on 17 August and invited the governor to visit him in Philadelphia (Williams, 104–5).

Thus, although the name was superseded, a political entity called the State of Franklin existed a century before there was a State of Washington, and seventy years before the creation of Washington Territory. Tennessee was admitted to the Union in 1796.

2. Franklin acknowledged the tribute in a letter to Webster on 26 October 1789. Webster, in his own advanced years, often recalled that Franklin had once told him "that he had been all his life detecting his errors and had been obliged often to change his opinions."

3. Franklin's reference is to *Proverbs* 28:15–27; "He that hateth covetousness shall prolong his days" (verse 16); "He that maketh haste to be rich shall not be innocent" (verse 20); and "He that hasteth to be rich hath an evil eye. . . ." (verse 22).

4. Jackson 1976–79, 5:181.

5. Another account, however, reports that the river excursion took place *after* the session adjourned for the day (Peters, 169).

CHAPTER 13. THE OLDEST DELEGATE

1. One of the proposals was a hoax, a pleasantry not intended to be taken seriously by the convention. It is Proposal 8, that the convention examine the "Scottish mode" of selecting judges.

2. Presidents Washington, Jefferson, Madison, Monroe, Jackson, Lincoln, Grant, Cleveland, Wilson, Eisenhower, Nixon, and Reagan were elected to second presidential terms after serving a full first term of four years. In 1940 and 1944 Franklin Roosevelt was elected to the presidency for third and fourth terms. In 1951, the Twenty-second Amendment limited the presidential incumbency to two terms.

3. See chapter 9, chronology for May 31.

4. The notes of delegate Robert Yates are an exception; he wrote that the Franklin amendment provided no "salary but the devotion of *his* time to the public service" (Farrand 1966, 1:89).

5. In eighteenth century America, freeholders owned *land*. The term did not include tenants who paid rent.

6. Pinckney's formal motion left a blank instead of specifying a definite minimum.

APPENDIX A. REMARKS WRITTEN BY FRANKLIN BEFORE DELIVERY

1. The correct number in the 1707 Act of Union was forty-five members in the Commons. Franklin made the mistake in the written text which Madison copied. Delegate Robert Yates, in his notes on Franklin's speech (Farrand 1966, 1:205) used the correct number.

APPENDIX C. NOTE ON FRANKLIN'S USE OF A SEDAN CHAIR AT THE CONSTITUTIONAL CONVENTION

1. Franklin's sedan chair has become such a colorful stage prop in the annals of the federal convention that it appears routinely in current historical novels—in Michener's *Legacy* and Roberts' *Tidewater Dynasty*, for example.

References Consulted

Adams, Charles Francis, ed. 1856. *The Works of John Adams*. Vol. 1. Boston: Little, Brown.

Adams, James T., ed. 1940. *Dictionary of American History*. New York: Scribners.

Alden, John R. 1984. *George Washington*. Baton Rouge: Louisiana State University Press.

Aldridge, Alfred Owen. 1965. *Benjamin Franklin, Philosopher and Man*. Philadelphia: Lippincott.

Allison, Andrew M., *The Real Benjamin Franklin*. Salt Lake City, Utah: The Freeman Institute.

Alsop, Susan Mary. 1982. *Yankees at the Court*. New York: Doubleday.

Babbidge, Homer D., ed. 1967; *Noah Webster: On Being American*. New York: Praeger.

Bailyn, Bernard. 1967. *Ideological Origins of the American Revolution*. Cambridge: Harvard University Press.

———. 1986. *The Peopling of British North America*. New York: Knopf.

Bancroft, George. 1884. *History of the Formation of the Constitution of the United States of America*. 2 vols. New York: Appleton.

Beard, Charles. 1935. *An Economic Interpretation of the Constitution*. New York: Macmillan.

Berns, Walter. 1985. *The Writing of the Constitution of the United States*. Washington, D.C.: American Enterprise Institute.

Berstein, Richard B. 1987. *Are We To Be A Nation?* Cambridge: Harvard University Press.

Berthoff, Rowland. "A Country Open for Neighborhood." *Indiana Magazine of History* 84 (March 1988): 37.

Best, John Harden, ed. 1962. *Benjamin Franklin on Education*. Classics in Education, no. 14. New York: Teachers College, Columbia University.

Block, Seymour Stanton. 1975. *Benjamin Franklin: His Wit, Widsom, and Women*. New York: Hastings House.

Bloom, Sol. *The Story of the Constitution*. 1937. Washington: United States Constitution Sesquicentennial Commission.

Boardman, Roger Sherman. 1934. *Roger Sherman*. Philadelphia: University of Pennsylvania Press.

Bowen, Catherine Drinker. 1966. *Miracle at Philadelphia, May–September, 1787*. Boston: Little, Brown.

———. 1974. *The Most Dangerous Man in America*. Boston: Little, Brown.

Brant, Francis B., and Henry V. Gummers. Undated. *Historic Philadelphia*. Philadelphia: Corn Exchange National Bank.

Brant, Irving. 1950. *James Madison, Father of the Constitution, 1787–1800;* New York: Bobbs-Merrill.

Brown, Richard L., Stephen Betein, and Edward C. Carter, eds. 1987. *Beyond Confederation*. Chapel Hill: University of North Carolina Press.

Brown, William Garrott. 1905. *The Life of Oliver Ellsworth*. New York: Macmillan.

Burns, James MacGregor. 1982. *The Vineyard of Liberty*. New York: Knopf.

Burress, Richard. 1987. *We the People*. Stanford: Hoover Institution.

Bushman, Richard L. 1966. On the Uses of Psychology: Conflict and Conciliation in Benjamin Franklin. *History and Theory* 5 : 225–40.

Canfield, Leon, and Wilder, Howard. 1950. *The Making of Modern America*. Cambridge: Houghton Mifflin.

Carson, Rachel L. 1951. *The Sea Around Us*. New York: Oxford.

Carter, James D. 1955. *Masonry in Texas*. Waco: Grand Lodge.

Ceremonies at the Unveiling of the Statue of Benjamin Franklin. 1989. Philadelphia: Allen, Lane, and Scott.

Clark, Ronald W. 1983. *Benjamin Franklin: a Biography*. New York: Random House.

———. 1985. *Works of Man*. New York: Viking.

Cohen, I. Bernard. 1985. *Revolution in Science*. Cambridge: Harvard University Press.

Collier, Christopher, and James Lincoln Collier. 1986. *Decision In Philadelphia*. New York: Random House.

Commager, Henry Steele. 1987. The Achievement of the Framers. *This Constitution*, no. 15, 33–36.

Commager, Henry Steele. 1938. The Constitution: Was It an Economic Document? *American Heritage* 10.

Commager, Henry Steele. 1978. *The Empire of Reason*. New York: Anchor/Doubleday.

Connor, Paul W. 1965. *Poor Richard's Politicks*. New York: Oxford Press.

Corwin, Edward Samuel. 1956. Franklin and the Constitution. *Proceedings of the American Philosophical Society* 100 : 283–88.

Coulter, E. Merton. 1987. *Abraham Baldwin*. Arlington, Va.: Vandermere Press.

Country Beautiful, ed. 1973. *The Most Amazing American: Benjamin Franklin;* Waukesha, Wisconsin.

Cousins, Margaret. 1952. *Ben Franklin of Old Philadelphia*. New York: Random House.

Crane, Verner W. 1954. *Benjamin Franklin and a Rising People*. Boston: Little, Brown.

Davis, David. "The Significance of Excluding Slavery from the Old Northwest in 1787." *Indiana Magazine of History* 84 (March 1988): 75–79.

Donovan, Frank. 1962. *The Benjamin Franklin Papers*. Norfolk: Dodd, Mead.

———. *Mr. Madison's Constitution*. New York: Dodd, Mead.

Dyer, Thomas G. 1985. *The University of Georgia*. Athens: University of Georgia Press.

Emerson, Barbara Hesse. 1976. Franklin. *The Green Scene,* March.

Eiselen, Malcolm R. 1928. *Franklin's Political Theories*. Garden City: Doubleday.

Emery, Noemie. 1976. *Washington*. New York: Putnams.

Farrand, Max. 1921. *Fathers of the Constitution*. New York: Yale Press.

———. 1913. *The Framing of the Constitution of the United States*. New Haven: Yale University Press.

Farrand, Max, ed. 1966. *Records of the Federal Convention*. Rev. 4 vols. New Haven: Yale University Press.

Fay, Bernard. 1929. *Franklin, the Apostle of Modern Times*. Boston: Little, Brown.

Fay, Bernard. 1935. *Revolution and Freemasonry, 1660–1800*. Boston: Little, Brown.

Ferris, Robert, ed. 1976. *Signers of the Declaration*. Washington: U. S. National Park Service.

Ferris, Robert G., and James H. Charleton. 1986. *Signers of the Constitution*. Arlington, Va.: Interpretive Publications.

Fleming, Thomas, ed. 1972. *Benjamin Franklin, A Biography in His Own Words;* New York: Harper & Row.

Fleming, Thomas. 1971. *The Man Who Dared the Lightning: A New Look at Benjamin Franklin*. New York: Morrow.

Ford, Edward. 1946. *David Rittenhouse: Astronomer and Patriot*. Philadelphia: University of Pennsylvania Press.

Hanna, William S. 1964. *Benjamin Franklin and Pennsylvania Politics*. Stanford: University Press.

Haraszti, Zolten. 1964. *John Adams and the Prophets of Progress*. New York: Grosset and Dunlay.

Hindle, Brooke. 1956. *The Pursuit of Science in Revolutionary America*. Chapel Hill: University of North Carolina Press.

Historians of the Independence National Park, National Park Service. 1987. *1787: A Day-to-Day Story of the Constitution*. New York: Exeter Books.

Hixon, Richard F. 1968. *Isaac Collins*. New Brunswick, N. J.: Rutgers University Press.

Hopkins, Joseph, ed. 1964. *Concise Dictionary of American Biography*. New York: Scribner's.

Hunt, Gaillard, and James Brown Scott. 1920. *Debates of the Federal Convention of 1787*. New York: Oxford Press, for the Carnegie Endowment for International Peace.

Hutson, James H. 1987. New Documents *This Constitution,* no. 15, 27–32.

Jackson, Donald, ed. 1976–1979. *The Diaries of George Washington*. Charlottesville: University of Virginia Press.

Jacobs, Wilbur R., ed. 1976. *Benjamin Franklin: Statesman-Philosopher or Materialist?* Huntington, N. Y.: Krieger. (Excerpts from writings of Van Doren, D. H. Lawrence, Parrington, Saint-Beuve, Williams, and others.)

Jensen, Merrill. 1964. *The Making of the American Constitution*. Huntington, New York.

———. 1950. *The New Nation*. New York: Random House.

Jillson, Calvin C. 1981. Constitution Making: Alignment and Realignment. *American Political Science Review* 75:598–612.

Johnson, Allen, and Maline, Diemas, eds. 1931. *Dictionary of American Biography*. New York: Scribners.

Jones, Frank B., ed. 1982. *Ben Franklin Remembered*. Bloomington: Benjamin Franklin Guild.

Jones, Robert F., ed. 1978. *Formation of the Constitution*. Huntington, New York: Krieger.

Kammen, Michael. 1986. *A Machine That Would Go of Itself: The Constitution in American Culture*. New York: Knopf.

Kennedy, Roger G. 1985. *Architecture, Men, Women, and Money in America, 1600–1860*. New York: Random House.

Ketcham, Ralph L. 1966. *Benjamin Franklin*. Great American Thinkers Series. New York: Washington Square Press.

———. 1965. *The Political Thought of Benjamin Franklin*. Indianapolis: Bobbs-Merrill.

Ketchum, Richard M. 1950. *The Revolution*. New York: American Heritage Publishing Co.

Keyes, Nelson B. 1956. *Benjamin Franklin: An Affectionate Portrait;* Garden City: Hanover House.

Klein, Randolph Shipley, ed. 1986. *Science and Society in Early America*. Philadelphia: American Philosophical Society. Contains Esmond Wright, "Benjamin Franklin: The Old England Man" (39–56), and Edwin Wolf II "Frustration and Benjamin Franklin's Medical Books" (57–92).

Kristol, Irving, and Nathan Glazer, eds. 1987. The Constitutional Order, 1787–1987. *The Public Interest*, no. 86 (special issue).

Kurlund, Philip B., and Ralph Lerner. 1987. *The Federal Constitution*. 5 vols. Chicago: University of Chicago Press.

Langguth, A. J. 1988. *Patriots*. New York: Simon and Schuster.

Lemay, J. A. Leo, and P. M. Zoll, eds. 1986. *Benjamin Franklin's Autobiography, Authoritative Texts, Backgrounds, Criticism*. New York: Norton.

Levy, Leonard W., ed. 1986. *Encyclopedia of the American Constitution*. 4 vols. New York: MacMillan. (Article on "Franklin" by Dennis J. Mahoney.)

Levy, Leonard W., and Dennis J. Mahoney, eds. 1987. *The Framing and Ratification of the Constitution;* New York: MacMillen.

Lingelbach, William B. Benjamin Franklin and the American Philosophical Society in 1956. *Proceedings* 100:354–68.

Lopez, Claude-Anne. 1981. *Benjamin Franklin's 'Good House'*. Washington: Superintendent of Documents.

Lopez, Claude-Anne, and Eugenia W. Herbert. 1975. *The Private Franklin: the Man and his Family*. New York: Norton.

Lucas, F. L. 1960. *The Art of Living: Hume, Walpole, Burke, Franklin.* New York: MacMillan.

Lyon, Hastings. 1936. *The Constitution and the Men Who Made It.* Boston: Houghton-Mifflin.

McCaughey, Elizabeth P. 1987. *Government by Choice.* New York: Basic Books.

McDonald, Forrest. 1985. *Novo Ordo Seclorum.* Lawrence: University of Kansas Press.

———. *Requiem.* 1988. Lawrence: University of Kansas Press.

McLaughlin, Andrew C. 1935. *A Constitutional History of the United States.* New York: Appleton.

———. 1967. *The Confederation and the Constitution.* New York: Collier.

Madison, James. 1966. *Notes on Debates in the Federal Convention of 1787.* Athens: Ohio University Press.

Maier, Pauline. 1987. The Philadelphia Convention and the Development of American Government. *Liberty's Legacy.* Columbus: Ohio Historical Society, 61–73.

Mee, Charles E., Jr. 1987. *The Genius of the People.* New York: Harper & Row.

Mencken, H. L. 1937. *The American Language.* New York: Knopf.

Miers, Earl Schenck, ed. 1956. *The American Story.* Great Neck, N.Y.: Channel Press. (See especially Whitefield J. Bell, "The Father of All Yankees," 67–74, and Irving Brant, "Establishing a Government," 93–98.)

Miller, Helen Hall. 1975. *George Mason: Gentleman Revolutionary.* Chapel Hill: University of North Carolina Press.

Mitchell, Broadus, and Louise Pearson Mitchell. 1964. *A Biography of the Constitution of the United States.* New York: Oxford University Press. 1964.

Moore, Virginia. 1979. *The Madisons.* New York: McGraw-Hill.

Morgan, Edmund S. 1956. *The Birth of the Republic.* Chicago: University of Chicago Press.

———. 1962. *The Gentle Puritan: Ezra Stiles, 1727–1795.* New Haven: Yale University Press.

Morison, Samuel Eliot, ed. 1923. *Sources and Documents Illustrating the American Revolution, 1764–1788, and the Formation of the Federal Constitution.* 2d ed. New York: Oxford University Press.

Morris, Richard B. 1987. *The Forging of the Union.* New York: Harper & Row.

———. 1986. *Witnesses at the Creation;* New York: Holt.

Morse, John T., Jr. 1899. *Benjamin Franklin.* American Statesman Series. Boston: Houghton Mifflin.

National Committee to Signalize Benjamin Franklin's Contribution to American Civilization. Undated. Organized by the Franklin Institute, Philadelphia. 3 vols., unpaged, mimeographed (examined in the Public Library, Louisville, Kentucky).

Nye, Russel Blaine. 1960. *The Cultural Life of the New Nation;* New York: Harper & Row.

Parton, James. 1971. *Life and Times of Benjamin Franklin.* New York: Da Copo Press (reprint).

Peters, William. 1987. *A More Perfect Union*. New York: Crown.

Pifer, Alan, and Lydia Bronte, eds. 1986. *Our Aging Society: Paradox and Promise*. New York: Norton. Contains Andrew Achenbaum, "The Aging of the First New Nation," 15–32.

Potter, John W. 1900. *A Century of American Diplomatic History—1776–1876*. Boston: Houghton Mifflin.

Powers, Deborah Stanley, ed. 1976. *Revolutionary America;* Bloomington: Lilly Library, Indiana University.

Ramsey, James G. M. 1967. *Annals of Tennessee;* Knoxville: East Tennessee Historical Society.

Randall, Willard Sterne. 1984. *A Little Revenge: Benjamin Franklin and His Son*. Boston: Little, Brown.

Rossiter, Clinton. 1964. *Alexander Hamilton and the Constitution;* New York: Harcourt, Brace; 372 pages.

———. 1953. *Seedtime of the Republic*. New York: Harcourt Brace.

———. 1968. *1787: The Grand Convention*. New York: Macmillan.

Russell, Phillips. 1926. *Benjamin Franklin: the First Civilized American*. New York: Brentano's.

Rutland, Robert A. 1987. *Well Acquainted with Books*. Washington: Library of Congress.

Sayre, Robert. 1964. *The Examined Self: Benjamin Franklin, Henry Adams, Henry James*. Princeton: University Press.

Schick, Frank L., ed. 1986. *Statistical Handbook on Aging Americans*. Phoenix: Oryx Press.

Schoenbrun, David. 1976. *Triumph in Paris: The Exploits of Benjamin Franklin*. New York: Harper & Row.

Schrag, Peter. 1964. *Ratification of the Constitution and the Bill of Rights*. Boston: D. C. Heath.

Seed, Geoffrey. 1978. *James Wilson*. Millwood, N. Y.: KTO Press.

Seldes, George. 1968. *The Great Quotations*. New York: Pocket Books.

Sheehan, Bernard. 1987. *The Northwest Ordinance*. Indianapolis: Indiana Historical Society.

Shoemaker, Ervin C. 1966. *Noah Webster: Pioneer of Learning*. New York: AMS Press.

Smith, Charles Page. 1956. *James Wilson*. Chapel Hill: University of North Carolina Press.

Stourzh, Gerald. 1969. *Benjamin Franklin and American Foreign Policy;* Chicago: University of Chicago Press.

Strayer, Joseph R., ed. 1939. *The Delegate from New York: Notes of John Lansing, Jr.* Princeton: Princeton University Press.

Thorpe, Francis Newton. 1891. *The Story of the Constitution;* New York: Chatauqua Press.

Tourtellot, Arthur Bernon. 1977. *Benjamin Franklin: His Boston Years;* Garden City: Doubleday.

U. S. Army. Center of Military History. 1986. *Soldier-Statesmen of the Constitution.* 16 booklets.

Van Doren, Carl. 1938. *Benjamin Franklin.* New York: Viking.

———. 1943. *The Great Rehearsal: the Story of the Making and Ratifying of the Constitution of the United States.* New York: Viking.

Walsh, James J. 1935. *Education of the Founding Fathers.* New York: Fordham University Press.

Warfel, Harry. 1936. *Noah Webster: Schoolmaster to America.* New York: Macmillan.

Warfel, Harry R., ed. 1953. *Letters of Noah Webster.* New York: Library Publishers.

Warren, Charles. 1967. *The Making of the Constitution;* New York: Barnes and Noble.

Williams, J. D. 1986. *The Miracle at Philadelphia.* Salt Lake City: University of Utah.

Williams, Samuel C. 1974. *The Lost State of Franklin.* Philadelphia: Porcupine Press.

Williams, Selma R. 1970. *Fifty-Five Fathers;* New York: Dodd, Mead & Co., 179 pages.

Wills, Garry. 1984. *Cincinnatus: George Washington and the Enlightenment.* Garden City: Doubleday.

Wilson Quarterly. 1987. "The Constitution" Vol. 12, no. 2. 96–156 (Articles by Peter Onuf, Jack Recove, A. E. D. Howard.)

Wood, Gordon S. 1969. *The Creation of the American Republic.* Chapel Hill: University of North Carolina Press.

Wright, Esmond. 1986. *Franklin of Philadelphia.* Cambridge: Harvard University Press.

Yates, Robert. 1987. *Secret Proceedings and Debates of the Convention. . . .* Albany: Webster and Skinner, 1821. (Reprint with a Foreword by John Charles Armor, edited by George R. Stewart; Birmingham Public Library.)

Zall, P. M., ed. 1980. *Ben Franklin Laughing.* Los Angeles: University of California Press.

Index

183